'Should I bring an umbrella?'

Umbrella phalanx protects Japanese tourists in Rome from a deluge.

In Taman Negara National Park in West Malaysia a boat with family on board glides silently downstream against a background chorus of cicadas, the occasional chatter of monkeys and the unmistakeable haunting cry of a circling eagle. With luck the wing-beat of a huge rhinoceros hornbill and its harsh laugh will be heard and you will spot it. It is early afternoon. The air is still. It is very hot. This timeless scene is in grave danger of becoming a rare sight in the tropics due to both legal and illegal forest clearance.

'Should I bring an umbrella?'

Celebrating weather in photographs

ALAN JOHNSTON

BOOKLINK

2009

This is Kilclief, Co. Down, just inside the entrance to Strangford Lough, basking in a perfect summer's day — but it could be a very different with wild waves from the open sea. St. Patrick sailed past here in 432AD before landing a few miles further into the lough. He is reputed to have made a place of Christian worship on the site of the little church in the foreground, still in regular use today. Beyond stands Kilclief Castle, built 500 years ago by the Anglo-Normans, the oldest of several such defensive tower-houses in the area. Generations of my family have played and bathed from this small safe beach.

Contents

The so-called 'feather beds' with churning foam at Portballintrae, Co. Antrim

To Phyl, my dearest love

Strangford

Acknowledgements

I have a long list of wonderful friends and family to thank for their encouragement and support in this enterprise intermittently over three years – and not forgetting some refreshingly candid comments! It would be invidious to mention by name more than a small handful beyond that one person, Phyl, to whom this book is dedicated.

The handful are: Professor Ronnie Buchanan for urging me to publish some of my photographs – and for kindly writing the Foreword; my very good friend Leslie McCullough whose cheerful support in times of technological crisis has, without a doubt, played an

essential role in helping this book to see the light of day; then there is
my book designer, Wendy Dunbar, whose guiding professionalism,
artistic hand and calming patience have done so much to bring things
together. And of course Dr Claude Costecalde, my publisher, who was
quick to see the potential of my unique angle on local and world
weather. To all these go my special thanks.

Finally, to my close family and to everyone else in Ireland and Britain
with whom I have been in contact over the years, I conclude with a big
thank you. And I also express my thanks especially to all those
magnificent Northern Ireland weather presenters on TV and radio. I
feel I know each one of them personally, but they do not know me and
how I daily hang on their every word – and then add my own local
twist!

ALAN JOHNSTON

Hail shower

Foreword

Not many of us would think of weather as a theme for the story of our life, unless perhaps we had worked as a professional meteorologist. And yet it fits Alan Johnston's book perfectly, the chronicle of a life lived in many places, recorded with the discerning eye of an artist and photographer for whom the sky in its infinite variety has been his canvas.

Both Alan and I are fortunate to live on the shores of Strangford Lough on Ireland's north-eastern coast, for this is one place where the pattern of weather and clouds changes constantly, often from hour to hour. Alan has many photographs which reveal the beauty of the Lough and its surroundings, but in this book he ranges across a wider world, for he in the course of his long life has travelled and worked in many places. In these pages we can follow him from Europe to the Middle East, to Africa and the Far East, and see their cities and countrysides and people through his eyes. The sky is always in his view, usually with clouds whose infinite variety adds colour and texture to his pictures – towering cumulus above a stormy sea, or mist clothing a forest in early dawn.

Landscapes predominate in this collection, from the green valleys and grey skies of the English Lake District to the dazzling white of the Swiss Alps, and the muddy greens of slow-moving rivers in the Malaysian jungle. Weather is the theme of the book, but there are people too, of every shape and colour and posture, not excluding the revealing portrait of the author himself in the opening pages. As readers, we are fortunate that someone had the foresight to give the young Johnston a Kodak Box Brownie as a Christmas present over seventy years ago. There have been other cameras in the intervening years, but the quality of the photographs has remained constant, initially enjoyed mainly by the family, but now made available to us all as well.

R.H. BUCHANAN

summer sunset from my skylight. The small dash of a contrail is of course
olluting the atmosphere, but it makes me wonder about all the people up
ere flying between N. America and UK or mainland Europe. Who are they?
Vhere are they going? Why? Are there bored kids wriggling around? And so on.
re people looking down at me? I hope they have noticed this gorgeous sunset.

Setting the scene

Allow me, please, as the author, to introduce myself. I am taking my ease on a bright spring day in an armchair dumped in a County Donegal bog. Just to clarify, it is the chair that is dumped, not me. Quite shamefully dumped too, like any litter, refuse, junk, trash or whatever you may care to call any eyesore that disfigures our beautiful landscape. Anything else you may wish to know about me should reveal itself through my photographs and my literary endeavours that follow.

Alan Stuart Johnston – lost in deep meditation?

Rain! Merely tiresome or plain exasperating? (Or the answer to prayers in some parts of the world?) 'Should I bring an umbrella?' is a question I am frequently asked by Phyl, my wife and No. 1 model. In response I usually err on the safe side, thus reinforcing my reputation of reliability beyond that of any professional weather forecaster. But they, like me, being human and thus fallible (like technology), are entitled to be wrong just occasionally, though not too often.

Without rain life for all of us would peter out. This is fact. As inconvenient a fact as the possibility of rain disrupting the big day, a wedding perhaps or that annual sports event or simply the day on which you had planned to cut the grass. What an endless catalogue of rain-related disappointments and frustrated human activities we can all list. Since we can do nothing to influence the daily weather pattern (as distinct from climate change) we might as well enjoy it and some of the misty beauty it can bring – such the view above.

A soft day, Kylemore, County Galway

These elephants in Thailand are prepared for rain – or sun

Contrast the photograph opposite with these desert sands blown into drifts that engulf all in their path and even occasionally leave a dusting of the Sahara as far north as my house by Strangford Lough.

I have been an intermittent and increasingly keen observer of weather for almost as long as I can remember. It interests me because of its infinite variety of forms, its effects on the daily lives of every living creature and on every plant. I especially love the beauty and excitement of ever changing skies and seasons. These daily displays of nature can be particularly spectacular in this north-western group of islands, Ireland, Britain and all the offshore islands, positioned between the vast Atlantic Ocean and continental Europe and midway between the arctic and the tropics.

As a photographer since the 1930s I have had the good fortune to have lived and worked for 25 years not only in our temperate lands but in tropical lands and desert lands – Middle East, Africa and Far East. Later my camera and I, accompanied by my model, visited a wide range of countries on holiday, and everywhere I have photographed the weather, though usually not consciously, while observing its impact on the local people living in a great range of climates.

I have chosen every photograph for this book to 'talk' in some way. Some shout. Some just whisper. Some may make you wonder what on earth is the weather connection, yet there always is a connection, however subtle. But above all it is a photographic celebration of weather, with some inevitable passing nods in the direction of escalating climate change. As a layman I set out in Chapter 6 some serious thoughts on this. Throughout the book my collection of photos and anecdotes comprise only the more pleasant, beautiful, amusing or thought-provoking things around us. Next is an example of a photo which I interpret for you in my own way, leaving most other photos for your interpretation.

A wintry Ballycastle beach, Co. Antrim, with the distinctive profile of Fair Head in the background and the Mull of Kintyre, Scotland, on the horizon. Corrymeela Centre, the peace and reconciliation community, sits behind the cliffs beyond the beach.

The message of this eye-catching cobbler's shopfront in Skerries, Co. Dublin, could be interpreted as 'Walk!' – both for the sake of your health and of the environment. The fact that the sign in the door says 'Closed' means he is either out for lunch or has gone for a walk! Maybe. Or the whole thing could conceivably be a literacy test for little kiddies …

Here now is a CONTENTS summary:

CHAPTER 1

Appreciating Irish Weather launches boldly into this apparently ludicrous approach to weather in Ireland which few can have dared to adopt. Perhaps you may be drawn towards my way of thinking when you read on and absorb my photographs.

The Ha'penny Bridge over Dublin's River Liffey on a sparkling February day.

Enjoying the sunshine outside Belfast's Palm House in the Botanic Gardens, a Victorian splendour.

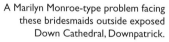

A Marilyn Monroe-type problem facing these bridesmaids outside exposed Down Cathedral, Downpatrick.

The familiar outline of the Mournes, Co. Down, seen across Dundrum Bay in winter.

CHAPTER 2

Similar Weather across the Water examines both
the similarities and some of the subtle differences
between the weather in Ireland and Britain.

ISLE OF MAN

A familiar cottage in
the north, snug against
the gales that blow off
the Irish Sea.

ENGLAND

A dramatic lenticular cloud seen beyond a pub in
the Pennines, a region where the topography not
infrequently leads to the development of such
clouds. People could be forgiven for having mistaken
these clouds for flying saucers.

WALES

Fog almost prevented us from
taking off from Belfast one
Christmas-time and when we
approached Liverpool over
the solid blanket, we were
treated to this silhouette of
the mountains of Snowdonia
in North Wales, bathed in
sunshine above the fog, like an
island in a stormy sea.

SCOTLAND

The dark sky of this autumn morning scene
in Dumfriesshire was not really as
threatening as it looked from an old friend's
house. I knew no umbrella would be needed
– as we would be in the car anyway.

CHAPTER 3

Everyone Else's Weather makes essential comparisons with weather and climates beyond our shores in those parts of the world I have seen, with some surprising experiences.

A dugout canoe in Malaysia slips peacefully by.

Criss-cross shade in Morocco. How dull a scene would be without shadows cast by the sun.

The shrub savannah near Maidugari in Northern Nigeria has magnificent bird life and huge termite mounds like this, its cathedral-like design acting as air-conditioning in the blazing sun.

Ice crystals

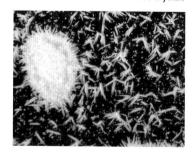

CHAPTER 4

Skiing on the Road to Damascus is in praise of the world's ice and snow in all its beauty and its climatic significance, through the lens of a photographer, really at heart a little boy who just loves the excitement of snow and ice, but who now has aged somewhat.

A brilliantly designed British telephone box adorned by snow.

The Mekong River delta in Vietnam receives a welcome annual flood, as shown here, essential for the cultivation of rice in the countless padi fields. Inundation by rising sea levels due to global warming would however be calamitous for such an area and for all who depend on it for their staple food. The main river is at the top of the picture.

CHAPTER 5

Elemental Forces and Climate takes a layman's look at some of these forces as I have encountered them, both at home and abroad, either directly or indirectly affecting climates, landscapes and all life.

Switzerland's Aletsch Glacier, the largest on mainland Europe, with Alpine choughs surveying their icy domain on a day of threatening weather.

CHAPTER 6

Energy from the Sun is a chapter looking at climate change and illustrating some alternative energies, past and future, and at a few of today's more dubious uses of energy, with hard truths to be faced and no easy answers.

Sunrise from my window is often enhanced in fine weather by contrails of transatlantic aeroplanes.

Wooden Roman water wheels and aqueducts like this one on the Orontes River near Hama in Syria were still in regular use when I worked in Syria and Lebanon in 1948–52. They are supremely functional and enduring.

CHAPTER 7

Enjoying the Weather brings a little light relief after the last chapter, often in the most surprising ways, agreeable photographic opportunities whether outside in the prevailing weather or indoors avoiding it.

Bicycles are an accepted way of transport in Copenhagen and come in many forms, often with trailers.

A Parisian gentleman catches up with the news outside the Louvre.

CHAPTER 8

Home Skies, Sea and More shares with you a unique combination of weather, seas, tides, farmland, wildlife and passing craft around the narrows by the entrance to Strangford Lough, County Down. I take you on a journey through all points of the compass and through the seasons, as seen from my house.

Sky and pladdies (rocky islands exposed at low tide) looking towards the Bar Mouth, Strangford Lough with the open Irish Sea beyond.

As low in the sky as a rainbow can be – looking north towards Portaferry, Co. Down.

CHAPTER 9

A journey from Box Brownie to digital is a brief look at my days behind a camera lens, a wild mix of successes, failures, adventures, indignities even – years of challenge and enjoyment.

Here therefore is a tiny fraction of a lifetime's fun with a camera – 83 years in front of a lens and over 70 behind one. I hope you will like this miscellaneous collection of weather-related world photos. The daily weather is all around us all to be enjoyed or to be tolerated despite adversities. Indeed we should be making the most of it by turning its many effects (sun, wind, waves, currents, and the rest) to our advantage. I dare to believe that you may even be persuaded to agree with me over the way I look at weather, though on some dreary winter's day you might just find that a wee bit difficult. On the other hand my photos and tales might help to brighten your day. I hope so – and so does my camera!

You might reasonably expect advice from me about whether or not to bring an umbrella but I fear I am only able to give negative advice. Do NOT bring an umbrella – if it is promptly going to be blown inside out; if you keep losing the things; if you are going for a sail; if you are about to trek across the Gobi Desert; if you are going to play snooker, football, tennis, or most other sports (except golf). It can help though, for a short term forecast, to be aware of the look of the sky and the movement of clouds, especially looking in the direction from which the wind is blowing. It does no harm too to pay some heed to the weather forecast, adjusting it to suit the kind of weather pattern with which you are familiar for your own micro-climate, which cannot possibly be taken into account in detail in 'official' forecasts. Showers are always hit-and-miss affairs and might fall on you while not a drop falls only a short distance away. And – not only does the English language have several names for rain (some unprintable!) but so also do other languages, while the Inuit have many names for snow. Even radio and TV forecasters will occasionally trip up over a tongue-twister in saying what weather we might expect for the day – and consequently get the giggles on air, for which my special thanks to Tomasz Schafernaker!

Oh yes, another point – my antennae have become accustomed to twitching when a shower threatens to soak the almost-dry washing on the clothes line. I take appropriate action, which Phyl greatly appreciates. Indeed this book could instead equally well have been called 'Should I Hang out/Bring in the Washing?'

Should you think some of the photos are wrongly captioned you will (I hope) be wrong, the explanation being that quite a few have been taken many years ago, since when the scene may have altered out of all recognition. Some photographs are therefore of historic interest. One aspect that has not changed however, is the Irish and British weather, which treats us to the same wonderful variety show – spring, summer, autumn, winter.

Finally, an apology to some readers. I am sorry that despite my lifetime's journeying I have not depicted in these pages your favourite spot on the globe, places such as Bulgaria, South America, Wigan, The Maldives, Finland, the South Pole, Auchtermuchty and St. Helena. Anyway I'll bet that most of the inhabitants of these and other places have never been to Ballygobackwards! But I have visited it, or at least somewhere like it – if I remember rightly …

Besides opening a hitherto blinkered weather eye you might also pick up a few photographic tips along the way and with a bit of luck you will find yourself hooked on the fascinating world of world weather, a natural phenomenon profoundly affecting us all, animals and plants alike. I like the 21st Century's simple injunction 'enjoy!'. So, **ENJOY!**

1

Appreciating Irish weather

Ireland stands four-square to the prevailing elements streaming in from the broad Atlantic and it is only the western coasts of Britain that are exposed in quite the same way as most of Ireland's shores, though there are no coasts in our islands that are not from time to time subjected to the fiercest of gales. Indeed, of all the most densely inhabited islands in the world, we are probably the windiest.

There was no wind this day but the trees tell of the fury of westerly Atlantic gales at Dunfanaghy, Co. Donegal. The ridge of Muckish lies beyond.

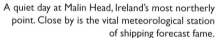

A surfers' paradise where the River Bush flows into the North Atlantic at Portballintrae. The Bush is famed not only for its fishing but for its Irish whiskey from Bushmills Distillery.

A quiet day at Malin Head, Ireland's most northerly point. Close by is the vital meteorological station of shipping forecast fame.

Now for the genial tones of the TV weather presenter, who is only doing his or her best, so be tolerant: 'Another deep depression is forming over the Atlantic that will affect us all during the coming weekend bringing heavy rain and strong to gale force winds.' Forecasts like this can be heard in any month but happily not too often in summer. All except surfers must groan 'here we go again.' Shipping forecasts reflect the same message in more detail covering a vast sea area around these islands perched on the fringe of continental Europe. Mariners fail to take note at their peril. Look for example at the photograph opposite of Malin Head on the far north-west corner of Co. Donegal on a relatively calm day – I value my life too much to attempt a photo from this spot in a gale.

Fishermen sorting out their nets at Cushendun, County Antrim, in a wild offshore wind.

I contend that it should not be left to surfers alone to rejoice, but that many of the rest of us might find the fast moving weather display less depressing, were we to observe more closely the ever-changing skies and follow the progression of the seasons around our small archipelago on the edge of a great ocean. Indeed our islands form one climatic unity with few if any comparable examples. Not only do our encircling seas govern our weather but they provide the thrill of thundering waves crashing onto rocks, or the stillness of a mirror reflecting the skies overhead, such as here.

Castlerock, Co. Derry; the sea mist seen against Co. Donegal in the background later rolled in.

In Ireland there is a marked difference in how wet it is between the east and the west, with the latter in places receiving at least three times the annual rainfall experienced in eastern coastal fringes. Sunshine too significantly favours the east. However the skies of the west and the quality of light can be especially dramatic both in how they look and how they move and trail their cloud shadows over the land.

Mountain ranges and valleys tend to create their own weather as winds are forced up and over them, so my top marks go to a mountain summit, not just in Ireland but anywhere in the world, as being the best place for appreciating weather. Those who go there are sure to associate a walk or a climb with the weather they experienced and the company they had on that day. As anyone who has climbed to the top of a ridge or a mountain top cannot have failed to notice, it is almost always much windier. It is wetter too. Rain, hail, snow can suddenly strike, blowing horizontally, with little warning. And it is of course colder, often much colder, hence the need for layers of appropriate clothing which could be literally life-saving, especially if clouds should roll in, even in apparently fine settled weather. The path up or the track down over rough terrain can be obscured by mist very quickly, leading to disorientation. Hence map, compass, whistle, food and drink are essential. So is an ear to that morning's weather forecast.

Dispersal of a blanket of cloud enveloping 2796 ft. Slieve Donard, the highest peak in the Mournes, which dominates the skyline of Newcastle, Co. Down. The Mournes might not be the highest of mountains but they provide challenging walks and climbs and when snow-capped in winter, sometimes for weeks at a stretch, their grandeur is excitingly enhanced.

The Mournes in winter, seen across Loughislandreavy. Slieve Donard on the left presents an unfamiliar profile.

A summit wreathed in cloud not only means no views of nearby peaks nor of the panorama spread out below, it also means no photographs, except maybe of ghostly shapes of friends nursing a reviving hot cup of tea, huddled close by cairn or boulder. But that is an occupational hazard of mountain climbers, walkers and photographers alike. Yet … a gap in the clouds may unexpectedly reveal, sometimes only for a few moments, views that make all the sweat and toil of the climb worth the effort. There is nothing to compare with the clear invigorating air of a peak to lift the spirits with views all around through 360 degrees. Some of my own mountain photos are included to give some inkling of how wonderful is the experience of achievement and of isolation from the rest of the world and how it feels to be right in the midst of the elements and of all they can throw at one. A friend used to say, when gazing up at some clouded peaks, 'the mountain gods are jealous today.' This meshes well with my own feelings on a summit, of something approaching a spiritual touch, like the presence of God.

From the depths of the sea to the top of a mountain fresh lobster would always be acceptable.

Walks along a shore with waves rolling in and hurling themselves onto the rocks in showers of spray, or cliff top walks, are as exhilarating in their own way as mountain climbs and are much more accessible to the very young and old alike. Without the risks posed by mountain climbing in bad weather, seaside, riverside and forest walks in such stormy conditions are usually of little risk provided simple commonsense precautions are observed. Such days of wild conditions can really blow away the cobwebs – and the cap from the head. Other serene days by the sea can be like one's idea of paradise.

A distinctly fresh day at Ballyhornan, Co. Down, with pots for crab and lobster out of reach of the waves.

With the endless changes of weather that we in the British Isles see, with all four seasons in one day sometimes, it is little wonder that it is a great talking point and indeed it helps to break the ice with people who are otherwise little more than strangers, so the topic therefore even has its social benefits. People from other countries are quietly amused at our apparent obsession with talking about the weather, for in many of them their weather pattern is so unchanging, often for months on end, that there is little worth saying about it. How boring!

Not only is our weather a conversation piece but any day can provide wonderful opportunities for photographers. Even a rotten day may provide just the nudge required for getting on with some long postponed indoors chore – perhaps fill that photo album? Or maybe the temptation to settle down in front of the fire with a good book. A sparkling day or a moody one on the other hand can entice me towards the great outdoors at any time of the year, being of an enviable age of having the time to indulge myself, be it in the garden, a walk, a row or a sail in my little dinghy, an exploration and much more, all providing wonderful photo opportunities.

Walk in the woods on a spring day in the National Trust's Castle Ward, Co. Down.

At this point I must make a confession, an apology even, of a sort, after one of those thoroughly miserable spells with day after day of muggy, drizzly weather during the summer holidays. Summer ought not to be like this – but it certainly can be. I thought how can I dare entitle this chapter 'Appreciating Irish Weather!' 'You must be joking', I can hear my friends muttering damply.

FAR LEFT
Midsummer's day sunset, Strangford Bay

LEFT
Western shore, Lough Neagh

The weather on the day I took this photo was disappointing at the time and yet it lent just the atmosphere I wanted. There are, though, days when the weather seems to get stuck in a rut of cold dry easterly winds that bring with them the sting of Siberia, when one is inclined to hunch the shoulders and button up the coat. Even so it can be eye-wateringly awful. It can occur in any month but it can be particularly hard to take when the heart yearns for the back end of winter.

A mid-1960s shot of a cottage in the west which must have seen all weathers. In the background there are traces of fields which have probably lain derelict since the Famine of the 1840s.

Yes, there really are some spells that are thoroughly dispiriting. Indeed there are days with weather that it is clearly quite impossible to enjoy – there is even the odd day that weather forecasters rightly describe as atrocious. However some disappointing days can display their own subtle beauty, with mists and curtains of rain transforming the landscape and seascape from time to time, raising hopes that this will at last turn out to be the clearing shower. The effects can be quite ethereal at times. Quite frustrating at others. But what would the patchwork Irish landscape be without its essential sprinkling from on high? Then comes the rainbow and renewed hope of an improvement.

Yet when the wind eventually shifts direction and the sun breaks through, one soon forgets what has gone before – so do not despair. Spring does eventually come and doesn't that early tentative sign of it put a spring in the step! Even if you may not notice it, the birds and the bees and the lambs in the fields will gradually proclaim the lengthening days. So will the familiar spring flowers in the garden, then the swelling buds in trees and hedges. As my mother used to say every year in her declining years, 'I just thank God that I am still alive to see another spring.' Amen to that.

Spring, summer – then autumn brings this

There are, in truth, few days so cold, so wet, so windy that one cannot venture out for a brisk walk, suitably clad. Or even a short spell of weeding and tidying in a sheltered corner of the garden, for the weeds do not go away of their own accord. Having plucked up the courage and made the effort to go out, it is generally not as bad as one imagined. One might even return home for a welcome hot mug of tea feeling vaguely virtuous and exercised, compared with those who opted for the warmth and comfort of the great indoors! Or have they just got more sense? There is no answer to that.

ugh Gill,
. Sligo, on a
of fast-
ving windy
owers and
nbows with
shine
ween them.

A vase of daffodils brings the colour of spring indoors.

ONE JULY DAY'S WEATHER IN IRELAND

You never quite know what the weather has in store. Read on! On the very day I was driving to hand over all the final text and photographs to my book designer, Wendy, I encountered the unexpected after leaving home in delightful warm and sunny weather. On my car radio at 2 pm I heard that 'there could be torrential and slow-moving thundery showers with localised flooding.' Some poor unfortunates, I thought. But then it all began to happen – to me. In Holywood, Co. Down, the downpour was such that upon arrival I could not set foot out of my car – just like Singapore in fact. My trusty emergency umbrella was in the car boot, but there was no point in trying to extract it as I would have been soaked to the skin in an instant. During a brief lull I dashed indoors for our meeting. Then there broke, almost overhead, one of the worst thunderstorms I have experienced in Ireland, with talk against the noise almost impossible at times. Flooding in Holywood was even featured in the evening TV BBC news.

TOP
Near Craigantlet before the storm broke

FROM LEFT
Kircubbin, near Ardkeen, Ballyhenry

With the benefit of hindsight I should not have been surprised as there had been an Atlantic low pressure system dominating our weather for a couple of weeks with a few hefty showers. During this spell anyone who looked at the sky would have been treated to one of the very best and constantly changing displays of beautiful and dramatic skies, with just about every type of cloud to be observed at one time or another, from cumulo-nimbus to early morning ground mists. In fact it was probably my favourite kind of weather, mostly warm and pleasant with gentle breezes and only the odd shower – just the thing for a landscape photographer.

On my way home after the meeting, a 30-mile drive along the Ards peninsula, to catch the ferry from Portaferry to Strangford, I saw a great succession of ominous skies with the occasional burst of rain. It was one of those times when the local remark 'the rain can't be far away' could quite justifiably have been used. Soon after I reached home, the sky became eerily black and menacing, then down came the inevitable torrents for a spell – see the photo below taken from my window. Finally, and rather apologetically, the late evening sun put in an appearance. Here are a few shots of that interesting day's weather, obviously laid on for me for daring to tackle this controversial subject, thus leaving myself open to occasional ridicule!

FROM LEFT
Ballywhite Bay; both sides of Strangford Lough at Portaferry; clouds building over Portaferry.

BELOW: Scene from a window as I dashed in through the door

IRISH HORSES

CLOCKWISE FROM LEFT
Serious horse-trading, Warrenpoint; Ballinasloe
horse fair; refreshments; Connemara ponies;
bath-time, Windmill Hill, Portaferry

Winter coat

MOUNTAIN SUMMITS

FROM LEFT
Benbulbin, Co. Sligo;
Croagh Patrick, Ireland's holy
mountain, Co. Mayo;
Slieve Donard from Murlough
Nature Reserve

FROM LEFT
Mweelrea mountain by
Killary Harbour,
Connemara; The
Twelve Pins viewed
across the stony
wastes of Connemara;
Nephin, Co. Mayo, seen
across Lough Conn

FROM LEFT
Distant Errigal,
Co. Donegal;
Muckish,
Co. Donegal,
from above
Magheraroarty
with inset of
the summit

Light and shade near Hilltown; spring snow on Slieve Binnian; essence of springtime, Slievenaman Road

ABOVE FROM LEFT

Snow shower at sunset; farmland behind Castlewellan

RIGHT

Low cloud base from Slievenaman Road

FAR RIGHT

Leitrim near Hilltown

IN AMONG THE MOURNES

Sun-burst over Tory Island from near Dunfanaghy

Tory Island in the N. Atlantic eight miles off the north coast of Co. Donegal. The north-east cliffs; looking westward along the hidden north coast. The views on my postcard show the striking profile of Tory from Dunfanaghy; the mysterious Tau Cross, hotel and church; Tormór entering the harbour; West Town with 6/7th century bell tower; cliffs and crystal clear seas on the dramatic east coast.

Rathlin Island, Co. Antrim, clockwise from left, showing sea stacks near Bull Point, a mecca for bird watchers; the Quay, looking back towards Ballycastle to which Rathlin is connected by ferry; view of the Manor House and the Harbour; St Thomas's Church and its historic graveyard.

Bull Point at the western point of Rathlin

TORY AND RATHLIN ISLANDS

CLOCKWISE FROM TOP LEFT

Ballintoy Harbour; the hidden bay behind Ballintoy Harbour with Sheep Island behind; above Ballintoy Harbour with Sheep Island and Rathlin beyond; Ballintoy Harbour from the air on a cold March day with an onshore wind; the sun does not always shine on Ballintoy where the cliffs take a pounding from the surf; Whitepark Bay, where the hedge is shaped by the wind and where Neolithic man lived.

BELOW FROM LEFT

The ridge of Lurigethan at the entrance to Glenariff; looking towards Cushendun from Torr Head Road as a shower approaches from beyond Glendun.

NORTH ANTRIM COAST

Ness Wood, a few miles from Derry City, after torrential rain produced a cappucino waterfall; wintry Sperrins across Glenelly Valley, Co. Tyrone; a peaceful corner of Co. Fermanagh by Lough Melvin with Co. Leitrim beyond.

HERE AND THERE IN NORTHERN IRELAND

Minnowburn Beeches, just four miles from Belfast city centre, seen here in all its autumn glory.

Down Cathedral shines above the fog, St. Patrick's grave lies inside the grounds.

Crom, Co. Fermanagh

Harvest shades above Belfast Lough and Holywood, Co. Down

Scrabo Tower – approaching touch-down at Newtownards airfield.

The ferry leaves Portaferry for Strangford, a five minute trip, avoiding a fifty mile journey around the lough. Behind the castle and the adjacent new RNLI station is the popular Exploris Aquarium.

Looking towards Marlfield on a balmy summer's day

Strangford Lough from Granagh Bay, with the Mournes in the distance

'Kindly Light' discharges crabs at Strangford harbo[ur]

BY STRANGFORD LOUGH

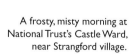

A frosty, misty morning at National Trust's Castle Ward, near Strangford village.

White-bellied Brent geese take off from Strangford Bay, maybe to their summer breeding ground in the Canadian Arctic.

THE NORTH-WEST

FAR LEFT
Mullaghmore, Co. Sligo

LEFT
Dartry Mountains, Co. Sligo

BELOW FROM LEFT
Looking north across a bleak Donegal Bay; a north Donegal farm; Owencarrow River, Co. Donegal, great for anglers

Cheery road workers

LEFT
Tranarossan Bay, Co. Donegal

35

COUNTY KERRY

CLOCKWISE FROM LEFT

Looking towards Sybil Head; an Atlantic shower approaches the Three Sisters; Coumeenole Bay from Slea Head, Dingle; Dingle cottage with the thatch well secured; who would dare disobey the STOP sign here in furthest Kerry

In 1967 I had the privilege (no longer possible) of visiting Great Blasket Island by curragh, here about to be launched at Drumquin Harbour on the mainland. Two Barrys (my son and my brother) went with me, rowed by islanders who had been amongst the remaining inhabitants who had left in 1953. Here is my photo-based watercolour of our curragh being launched, including scenes on and off the Blaskets.

Lough Leane, the Lower Lake, Killarney

North shore, Skerries, Co. Dublin

CENTRE LEFT

A fishing boat from Portacloy is dwarfed by Benwee head, Co. Mayo.

Johnstown, Co. Kilkenny has an air of tranquility while the pony eavesdrops.

Harvesting wrack in Connemara over fifty years ago

Curraghs, Renvyle, Co. Galway

HERE AND THERE
DOWN SOUTH

LEFT is Lurigethan near Cushendall in the glorious Glens of Antrim on a summer's day, with hedges bedecked with the crimson flowers of fuschia for months on end. Glenariff lies on the other side of the mountain while Glenballyemon is to its right. From the ridge of Lurigethan I have looked down at buzzards circling below me. The Mull of Kintyre in Scotland, not twenty miles off, seemed close enough to touch.

ABOVE is the famed Gap of Dunloe near Killarney in Co. Kerry on a wet autumn day, streams gurgling and mountains only dimly to be seen with, rising on the left, the Macgillycuddy's Reeks which include 3,414 ft. Carrantuohill, Ireland's highest peak. On the spring day my brother and I climbed it, with snow patches and little to be seen of the fabulous views, hot soup was extra welcome.

The weather depicted in these two contrasting photographs from the opposite corners of Ireland could just as easily have been reversed, with one weather scenario changing to the other, even within the hour. So don't be tempted to imagine it as always sunny in the Glens of Antrim and always wet in Co. Kerry! The latter, though, thrusting as it does into the Atlantic, naturally has a much wetter climate.

2

Similar weather across the water

'Across the Water' in Ireland means across the Irish Sea to Britain. There, being that little bit further from the moderating influence of the Gulf Stream and much closer to continental Europe's more extreme influence, there are significant weather differences. Yet both main islands of Britain and Ireland and all their offshore islands together enjoy the same basic climate package. Those same Atlantic gales that batter most of Ireland's coasts as they roar in from the west strike parts of Britain's coasts with no less ferocity at times, notably England's very exposed south-west and through the English Channel, much of Wales and a great part of Scotland's west and north. In listing these spots I in no sense belittle the fierce North Sea storms that assault Britain's east coast, leading to flooding and serious erosion.

Micro-climates exist in several parts of Britain as we will see. Indeed, if one follows national weather forecasts and not just the regional forecast, we seem to experience a selection of micro-climates right across the British Isles on any given day, with amazing variations from one corner to another.

Because of the proximity to the Continent with its higher summer temperatures, London and the south-east especially produce sweltering city streets and country lanes, every year eliciting the familiar tabloid

South Stack lighthouse near Holyhead, Anglesey, in Wales guides ferries to and from Dublin and Dun Laoghaire in all weathers. Every lighthouse around our coasts is now fully automated.

newspaper headline 'Phew What a Scorcher!' The English Midlands too can be very hot. But move towards the coasts and sea breezes bring welcome refreshment. East Anglia is much drier than western Britain and there are few places even in eastern Ireland to match it.

Four girls with four ice creams cool off on a hot summer's day on a Chester City tour bus.

Moving northwards into latitudes beyond any in Ireland, winters in the Scottish Highlands, notably the Cairngorms and the Grampians, usually have several months of sub-arctic climate, with skiing facilities to match. This helps to bring home the fact that the north of Scotland is on the same latitude as southern Norway. Indeed some of the Shetland Islands lie north of Bergen and Oslo, as well as Stockholm in Sweden and Helsinki in Finland.

The distinctive bulk of Slioch viewed from across Loch Maree in the North-west Highlands of Scotland on a fine spring evening.

Borrowdale

My remarks in Chapter 1 of the thrill of mountain tops, where weather is so often born, apply equally to all the big mountain chains in England, Scotland and Wales. The wettest place in England is in Borrowdale in Cumbria's incomparable Lake District – here is that lush valley depicted in benign mood.

LEFT: Glimpse from a window of Inverary Castle, home of the Duke of Argyll. Much of the magnificent castle in its imposing setting is open to be enjoyed by the public.

Phyl among the wonderfully weathered and mist-enshrouded Brimham Rocks in the Pennines.

Answer the following question: Is this (a) Concorde breaking the sound barrier? (b) Aliens from outer space approaching Planet Earth? (c) Cloud effect over Castletown, Isle of Man? No prizes for correct answer.

There is a curious thing about crossing the Irish Sea by ferry to Britain, and equally noticeable when arriving by air, that immediately upon arrival it strikes one as feeling 'different' in some indefinable kind of way and the weather encountered is a part of that feeling. Perhaps it is simply that one arrives in a new environment that is different from 'home'. Conversely, returning to Dublin, Belfast, Cork and other airports or arriving back at ferry terminals and launching out onto the open road, familiarity takes over and one is but a short drive from home.

A high speed ferry heads towards the setting sun en route from Stranraer to Belfast. Beyond is the familiar landmark of Ailsa Craig, the granite island from which come the curling-stones for that quintessentially Scottish sport of curling. A large colony of gannets nests there and in stormy weather some take refuge in the narrows of Strangford Lough.

The countryside of England, Wales and Scotland and the islands is so beautiful and so hugely varied that I hope you will enjoy my selection of photographs and will be able to think yourselves into the weather of the occasion. Especially look overleaf at the delightful small and historic city of Chester over the Christmas season. How the Romans must have found it an agreeable posting compared with the wild and windswept northern hills and moors through which they doggedly built their Hadrian's Wall, crossing Britain's narrowest point from east to west – or was it from west to east? Cheers.

Arriving by ferry in Birkenhead from Belfast I saw this ominous shower looming behind Liverpool's striking waterfront.
Apart from new constructions, the scene is very different from older times, since most of the harbour activity is now located further down the Mersey.

Talking of the Romans, what on earth would they have made of today's Londinium, and not least this view across the Thames, encompassing the London Eye alongside Shell Centre?

We now look at the prevailing weather when I shot the following photos over many years. I am splitting them between Scotland, Wales and England – and not forgetting the Isle of Man, but we start in Cheshire with the delightful city of Chester at Christmas.

It was the wettest, bleakest Christmas Eve in Chester but these friends were clearly enjoying their get-together.

BELOW LEFT: Bandstand by the River Dee
BELOW: Walking off lunch excesses

CHESTER AT CHRISTMAS

Eastgate Street

Christmas buskers

A heaven-sent Christmas morning in Grosvenor Park

FAR LEFT

Durham Cathedral dominates the River Wear beyond the winter tree tracery

LEFT

A chat in Shrewsbury's old Market Square on a brilliant day

Near Skipton in the Pennines this tree has been fashioned by the prevailing westerly winds.

Savill Gardens, Windsor Great Park, on a perfect Spring day

THE LAKE DISTRICT CUMBRIA

A shaft of light by Buttermere

Helvellyn summit in the spring. Scrutiny of the figures will spot one standing on his head – my brother-in-law John made a practice of doing this to prove he still had some energy left. His two sons possess the same genetic defect!

Wasdale Head with Scafell wreathed in cloud

onwy Castle near LLandudno, north Wales

Springtime in Powys

Niarbyl looking towards the Calf of Man at the southern tip

The Isle of Man in the middle of the Irish Sea gets every gale that blows but its beauty and enviable sunshine make up for this.

Llangollen and the River Dee on its course from Snowdonia to join the sea at Chester's weir

Point of Ayre at the north of the island

ISLE OF MAN   47

SCOTLAND

Gentle March sunshine lights up a glen in Argyll.

RIGHT: The Ayrshire coast bears the brunt of the westerlies that pile flotsam along the shore.

FAR RIGHT: Highland cattle won't be bothered by the approaching shower.

BELOW FROM LEFT

Loch Torridon in the north-west in May; spring green above the River Tweed; a centre for slate, Easdale in Argyll, with rain on the way – Easdale hosts world stone-skimming championships.

BELOW
A fierce gale from the unaccustomed east wrought havoc on this tree by Loch Lomond.

Ben Nevis, 4,408 ft., the highest peak in the Britsh Isles

LEFT: River Orchy with Ben Cruachan beyond – a hydro-electric source

49

3

Everyone else's weather

To look only at the weather in these islands would be to ignore what I consider three imperatives. Therefore, in this chapter, I show weather-related photographs from many places in the rest of the world. I think I can guarantee that some of them will surprise you.

An afternoon thunderstorm advances towards hill forest in West Malaysia and soon the air will be refreshed and every leaf and flower will be dripping when the rain moves on and the sun returns.

My first imperative to consider is this – a comparison of our climate with the climates of other lands across the world.   Because of the barbed jokes our maligned weather all too often invites, I believe it is important to make the point that our temperate climate is on the whole more benign than the climates of most other parts of the world. Their heat and cold are often too extreme for us and the occurrence of major disasters like droughts, floods, sandstorms and various forms of cyclone, typhoon or hurricane are part of the annual cycle to be endured. Yet I would be the first to agree that for a few weeks of the year many of these places beyond our shores are idyllic for a holiday, during which the drawbacks of, say, unending tropical heat and humidity, do not have a chance to pall. Consequently I am including examples of weather in some of the places abroad in which I have worked up to sixty years ago, or in spots where I have holidayed since retirement.

Hydra is a wonderful Greek island where there is no motor traffic and at night all one can hear is the occasional braying of a donkey and the ghostly 'pook' of many scops owls. The sunlight reflected off the bluest of seas can be blinding, like here below slopes carpeted with wildflowers.

Kyrenia in North Cyprus has a magnificent setting and is one of the most beautiful of harbours. The equally beautiful inset is a self-portrait of my left foot relaxing.

My second imperative asks: what makes our weather what it is? This raises the whole issue of the late-dawning realisation that people in virtually every spot on earth are currently, or soon will be, facing problems stemming from global warming. As we are all in this situation together and as climates everywhere are to a greater or lesser degree connected, we must accept that weather in the British Isles is increasingly going to be affected by occurrences thousands of miles away, not least the accelerating melting of the polar ice caps and the drastic shrinking of sea ice coverage.

My third imperative relates to global climates. There can surely be few remaining informed people who deny scientific evidence of global warming and its apparent bearing on catastrophic weather events in recent years. These events have in many cases have been worsened due to a combination of cyclical forces of nature exacerbated by man-made pollution, mainly in the form of carbon dioxide emissions. Some of the associated wholesale degradation of delicate eco-systems on land, in the seas and in the atmosphere has reached the point where it cannot be reversed, yet there remains much that can still be saved provided urgent measures are taken. Sceptics and ostriches please take note!

The so-called white villages just inland from the Costa del Sol in southern Spain feel a world away from the towns and villages and the rushing traffic along the coast road. This seems a timeless scene baking in the dry heat of a summer's day.

So in this chapter I share some of my images and experiences outside these very small islands of Britain and Ireland, hence my title 'Everyone Else's Weather' which is a touch misleading since I have not been literally everywhere, but I will do the best with what I have been fortunate enough to have seen over the years. Indeed this book would be incomplete without sharing some of my experiences with you, while giving you, I hope, some further idea of how things really look and how the people live in a wide range of places. Have a look at the next few diverse photographs for example.

Oriental umbrellas being made near Chiang Mai in Thailand's cooler northern highlands.

BOTTOM LEFT: In 1949 most of the houses in Khan Sheikhoun, Syria, were made of mud and straw keeping them relatively cool in summer and warm in winter – environmentally ideal.

BELOW: A bus in an Ethiopian village fills up with people and goods before setting off, while normal life goes on around it. The shamma, a loose cloak, is worn by both sexes. The ubiquitous eucalyptus trees, seen here, were successfully introduced in the late 1800s to replace the native juniper, virtually wiped out for timber exports.

A procession of young Buddhist monks in a Bangkok temple complex

So therefore, the theme running through these images is how climate and weather influence every person on the planet, though they have probably never paused to think about it. Why should they? They accept what is normal life for them and always has been. But consider: what they wear, the type of house they live in, the crops they grow, their very temperaments and so much else besides are dictated by where they live in the world and its climate. I therefore believe that for a better appreciation of how we in these north-western European islands are blessed with the climate we have (hard as that may be to accept at times!) it is essential to include in this book about our own weather, photographs and stories from abroad to achieve what I believe to be some measure of balance.

While I was living abroad I seized every opportunity of work travel. I travelled mainly by road but also often by air. This latter was a very relaxed affair compared with the security-bedevilled flying of recent times and its tedious airport queuing and waiting. Frankly, though considerably slower, flying was more enjoyable then, albeit a trifle adventurous at times. My happy hunting grounds included the Middle East with its varied climates from deserts to snowy mountains; hot and humid West Africa; the delightfully comfortable highlands of Ethiopia; and the cities and tropical rainforests of the Far East, in parts of which seasonal changes are barely discernible and the heat is unrelenting, unless one heads for the hill stations above about 4000 feet, where one feels immediately reinvigorated.

I cannot claim to have reached any significant mountain summits outside Britain and Ireland but there are a few that really do live on in the memory. One such is the 6400 ft. summit of Mount Olympus, the highest peak in Cyprus, which I hiked up with a Cypriot friend by the light of a full moon to see the sun rising over the distant Lebanon range and Mount Hermon, visible far to the east.

A huge contrast was by jeep to the top of Mount Washington in New Hampshire, USA, which claims the dubious distinction of having the worst weather in the world, including the highest ever recorded wind speed of 231 mph, in which even staggering on foot would have been a sheer impossibility.

One other memorable sight was from a jet flying from Karachi to Calcutta at dawn when the whole length of the Himalayas could be discerned, a rare unclouded sighting, said our pilot. This sight is only engraved on the mind, not on film. Such events are truly unforgettable.

This is the weather station that recorded that phenomenal wind speed on Mount Washington – taken on a relatively balmy day of 25 degrees F (minus 5C). The heavy chains anchoring the building to concrete moorings are not just there for decoration.

Aside from countries abroad in which I have lived, I have been to a wide range of countries either on business or, in more recent years, family visits or holidays. Some of these occasions have naturally only given time for a fairly superficial look around, though usually sufficient to gain some impression of the place, the people and the climate. Photographs during such brief visits have had of necessity to reflect the weather of the season in which I happened to be there. Mostly it was good weather because when planning holidays I always try to target seasons of normally reliable weather. One such success was New England in the fall. Sometimes however, the weather went awry, as in Morocco early one May when rain, snow and cloud totally obscured the Atlas Mountains as we crossed them from Marrakech. But I put that down to the vagaries of weather and had to give the camera a rest. Once we were south of the Atlas however, we soon dried out in the sun and Africa looked more like Africa, its inhabitants more as one would expect, instead of bedraggled wet camels, unhappy caparisoned horses and warmly cloaked Arabs and Berbers. Win some, lose some!

Tourism is vital in many economies. Here at Morocco's Ait bin Haddou local donkey and mule owners benefit from an unexpected flood in a wadi, by transporting visitors across without getting their feet wet, while a tempting display of local goods awaits them on the other side.

Just as in Morocco, wherever one is in the world there are times when the weather seems to be set resolutely against one and it can happen in places where one least expects it. Human nature being what it is, it can be most disappointing, annoying, frustrating ... One can only make the best of things and use any alternative occupations that may be on offer. Such as shops for all ages of boys and girls! And if retail therapy is not to your taste there is surely some culture, for instance, awaiting you.

Perhaps this lady at Copenhagen Airport has been looking for the very thing for her holiday in the sun.

A popular shop in Paris – or rather a man would be very popular with his wife, partner, or girl friend if he bought her a little something here!

Here is Italy's delightful Riva del Garda in the rain.

And here now is one of the many stunning views from nearby Monte Baldo when the weather finally turned up trumps.

One such disappointing occasion for me was in late October on my first visit to Lake Garda. I had hoped for opportunities to photograph and paint scenes of blue lake, fleecy clouds over mountain crags and sparkling Italian villages. Alas no. We experienced a week of an unrelenting blend of murky low cloud and rain, rain, rain, with mountains a vague outline at best and the sun a mere memory. Sales of umbrellas soared. Yet, as a photographer, I rejoiced in the wonderful moody effects, wet roads providing great reflections with the brightly painted buildings standing out with a vibrancy not always appreciated when everything else around is bathed in sunshine and all seems equally dazzling. High above, wispy clouds clung mysteriously to dizzying slopes like veils, all very atmospheric and some compensation for the rain and haze.

However there came a bonus of sheer joy. On our final full day the clouds lifted, the sun shone and the mountains, cliffs and valleys all around appeared in all their splendour, the peaks capped with the first fresh snow of the season. It was dreamtime for a landscape photographer, especially after a funicular ride to the snow line at some 6000 feet where the air was like vintage champagne and the skies all around gave constantly changing delight, proving that weather is a never ending variety show of indescribable beauty. It was worth the wait.

Obviously that bad weather was not typically Italian, even fringing the Alps. However my mental image of some countries and their inhabitants has often been reinforced by weather I experienced, for example the brisk far northern air on a day trip from Belfast to Reykjavik in Iceland with a friend is clearly imprinted on the mind. So was a day visit to Bergen in Norway in similar conditions. Then at the other extreme of climate scale, the atmosphere in Oman for a few days one January fulfilled my highest expectations, not least thanks to having a friendly personal introduction and to the weather turning up trumps.

It is only a short flight from Britain and Ireland to the fascinating ancient port of Bergen and this view from a snowy mountain top overlooking the town where my good friend Leslie and I saw all four seasons in one day.

However I would not dream of going there on holiday nor anywhere else in Arabia during the searing heat of summer, widespread air-conditioning notwithstanding. This latter adjunct to modern living in so many lands makes life bearable for those who have access to it, but it can be surprisingly chilly and dehydrating and the shock of emerging into an oven-like street can take one's breath away. A similar experience can be felt when stepping out of the relatively comfortable 'climate' of a modern aircraft into the real world outside, be it torrid or freezing. I gasp, and wonder how people can endure this heat and humidity all year round. Yet I have done it myself when younger – but advancing years make such extremes less tolerable.

Looking across a dry wadi towards a village inland from Muscat, Oman, where the surrounding date palms are flourishing and the January warmth was delightful.

This corner in Rangoon, Burma (now Myanmar), was bleak indeed in the monsoon.

In this 21st century we have global communications, global economy, global travel, global this and global that, but above all, we now realise, we have global weather. We cannot turn the clock back a few decades or a few centuries so we must adapt to living in our day and plan how to combat climate change over the centuries ahead. It will take the best of human brains, ingenuity and cooperation to arrive at workable solutions with extreme urgency. These solutions will hurt some more than others, but for an overall global survival plan to succeed everyone has some part to play.

By contrast this is the splendid Shwe Dagon Pagoda, Rangoon, where the tiled floor was too hot for my bare feet.

The TV tower in Prague in the Czech Republic not only provides global communications links but affords wonderful panoramas of that beautiful city and its many treasures. It is known locally as the Baby Tower because of the striking sculptures of babies climbing its exterior. It deserves to be better known by tourists.

This is a 1948 photo of the step pyramid at Saqqara, a few miles south of Cairo and now a UNESCO World Heritage Site. It is believed to be the world's oldest large stone structure, 200 ft. high, and was built as a Pharaoh's tomb around 2600BC by one of Egypt's most famous architects. As recently as 2009 further significant archaeological discoveries have been made at Saqqara.

Because of geography some measure of natural interdependence between countries has always existed, a prime example being the River Nile which flows northwards into the Mediterranean through Egypt's Nile Delta. Most of the flow of that great river originates in the Ethiopian Highlands via the Blue Nile and the Atbara rivers which join with the White Nile in Sudan. The White Nile flows from Lake Victoria at Jinja in Uganda, though Kenya and Tanzania also border Lake Victoria. It was the annual Nile flood, bringing rich sediments from mountainous Ethiopia, that contributed to the wealth of past Egyptian civilisations. The Aswan High Dam in Egypt (which began filling Lake Nasser in 1964) has been built to control the floods and to generate hydro-electricity for most of the country. However an unintended consequence has been the loss of the rich natural sedimentary deposits along the river and in the Nile delta, necessitating the use of artificial fertilisers. The annual run-off of sediments is instead gradually filling the vast Lake Nasser above the dam, thus reducing the capacity of the lake to hold water. Further, the reduced flow of fresh water from the Nile has affected fishing in the Mediterranean and altered nearby coastlines. It is a complicated and worsening situation – but it is now being tackled.

All too often there is brought graphically to our attention some natural disaster – flood, drought, hurricane, earthquake and the rest, but above all famine and disease – bringing ruination to thousands of unfortunate people somewhere across the globe. We see and hear this news, even while it is actually occurring, repeated almost ad nauseam on our TV screens and on radio and we read of it in newspapers. Whilst there can be an inclination to reach for the OFF button, this coverage of a global catastrophe can be absolutely invaluable in encouraging countless people to reach into their pockets. This is fact, not preaching, and if proof were needed look at the annual BBC Children in Need Appeal and the increasing yearly sums it raises.

A future Ronaldo?
Or maybe an Einstein?
Why not?

This must be one of the best examples of the usefulness of one of the 'globals', namely global communications, helping to come to the rescue of those in a desperate plight. In the days before our instant communication such disasters happened without our learning about them for perhaps weeks, months or maybe not at all. Today's escalating climate change, a combination of natural cyclical occurrences and manmade pollution, is bringing more disasters and of greater intensity. There is no escaping these.

My photographs have no news value in themselves – indeed not one of them has any 'shock horror' content, yet I enormously admire those photographers, reporters and others who daily risk their lives to bring us their stories of human suffering. My approach is instead to share with you via my lens and my stories the beauty and interest of a number of countries and their inhabitants living their daily lives. But my weather thread runs throughout in one guise or another, perhaps not always too apparent. See what you think of these images from a mix of countries across much of the world. Meanwhile, what future lies in store for this happy little footballer being laughingly pursued by his mother in a side street in Hua Hin, Thailand?

SNEAKING A QUICK LOOK INTO THE JUNGLE

Millipede

The word jungle conjures up an exciting image, but the reality of what I experienced, mainly in the tropical rain forests of West Malaysia, far exceeded my expectations. All the senses are brought into play but especially what one can see and hear and smell and touch. There is an extraordinary range of plants and creatures in these wonderful forests and even today we do not know what forms of life beneficial to mankind still remain to be discovered. Here is a photo of a large and beautiful millipede. Taman Negara, the National Park in the centre of the Malaysian peninsula, is particularly thrilling, but so too are the hill stations as here at Gunong Brinchang above Cameron Highlands with their own, mostly different, flora and fauna. So too are the great lowland forests running down to the almost eerie world of the coastal mangrove swamps. Lower left is an old photo of an eminent scientist lost in concentration in a mangrove swamp.

Mangroves

My first interest in going into the jungle was bird watching but soon one becomes hooked on all the other sights and sounds that envelop one and when walking along a track it is hard to know whether to be looking up or at the ground or to right or to left. Wherever one looks inevitably one misses something of interest. But consider the atmosphere. It is hot and humid and if it rains, which it most certainly often does, it can become surprisingly chilly and it becomes muddy and slippery under foot.

Gunong Brinchang

The best time to be in the jungle is around dawn when it is often misty and all is cool and refreshed and the air is filled with bird song and, depending on what type of jungle it is, there are other sounds that rend the air – above all is the whoop-whoop-whooping sound of the siamang gibbon, spine-chillingly thrilling to hear at the hill stations. At that time of day too one's chances of seeing wild boar, deer of several kinds and other mammals is much greater than later.

Little breeze can be felt at ground level below the layers of vegetation, with many forest giants attaining 150 feet, some even 200 feet. Trees like this will have started life perhaps in a rotting log, like this seedling tree. Around noon all seems still except for the scratchy sound of cicadas until, quite unexpectedly, monkeys or gibbons might spot you and hurtle away, crashing through the trees with breathtaking agility, uttering indignant cries. In Singapore Botanic Gardens I once came within a whisker of having my camera snatched and transported for ever to the treetops – as

the little so-and-so grabbed my precious Kodak Retina IIIc I spotted movement out of the corner of an eye and grabbed the camera. Picnic things were scattered as I won the tug-of-war with a macaque monkey and his pals.

There is little sign of bird life around the middle of the day. There are though a few birds to be seen and heard, notably the so-called brain fever bird (a cuckoo), whose endlessly repeated call on jungle fringes could drive one to distraction. But one of the most haunting bird calls is *taptibau* repeated several times ringing out, loud, clear, melodious, from the long-eared nightjar which energetically hawks for insects for just half an hour around sunset and sunrise. They often compete with the noisy croaking of frogs, especially after rain. Many are the bird songs and sights but the hardest birds to spot are the trogons as they are not only brilliantly camouflaged, but they are also silent and nocturnal; only once did I spot one perching motionless in the fork of a tree by day. The camouflage adopted by

creatures of the jungle is infinitely varied and mimicking. However I cannot possibly give you a catalogue of all I have seen except for a few more glimpses. Butterflies and moths abound. Here are moths which became entangled in a night bird-ringing net. No one has been able to identify the large one for me. Indeed, if only I had played my cards differently I might conceivably have had a worm named after me (what fame!) for I had spotted a 22-inch worm and mentioned it to a university zoologist. He informed me that it was suspected that such large worms existed in the area in which I had found it, but that none had ever been seen, though they were found in Australia. I photographed it but it just looks like a perfectly ordinary worm with my pencil for scale, so there is no point in showing it to you.

Some people would associate the rain forest with dangers and whilst of course there are pests like tiny biting insects, mosquitoes, fire-ants and leeches (which are pretty disgusting) there are few dangerous snakes, for example, and even they would normally only be a risk if accidentally trodden on. Far more dangerous are hornets, so one must take care not to brush against a nest near ground level. Dangerous too can be huge bees' nests, particularly should they be under attack by birds partial to honey, like the honey-buzzard, as you pass close by.

In some areas of West Malaysia there were – and I hope still are – some tigers. Here is a photo of Deirdre and a Malay guide studying prints of a female and cub on a river sandbank in Taman Negara. On the previous evening we had had a fairly close encounter with a tiger. We had been taken by boat at evening up a tributary of the main river to spend a few hours in a tree hide. There we all sweated mightily and insects had a field-day yet the four children remained wonderfully silent, no doubt with the greatest difficulty. We saw a few small animals but nothing really exciting – until we heard the double roar of a tiger, frustrated that our presence was scaring off its potential prey, said our guide.

Then silence. Eventually we had to let one of our two guides take the youngest kids back to the waiting boat, leaving three of us with the second guide. Nothing more of note happened, so we climbed down and made our way cautiously, and very much on our guard, in the dark along a narrow path towards the boat. Suddenly there was the most appalling roar and it went on and on and on – until our jangling nerves realised that it was just our outboard motor starting up a few hundred yards away! We had not finished up as tiger supper after all. (Phyl later took up the making of plaster casts of animal spoors, now in our attic – but that was after this rare tiger opportunity unfortunately.)

As for elephants, many times we have seen dung and footprints as evidence of elephants, sometimes very fresh, and we have heard them. So, at this point let me tell you the fascinating 'Story of a Nut' (as told to me by the nut):

– *I am a fruit ripening contentedly in the sun on a forest tree, safe among all the dense foliage*
– *along comes a huge elephant which wraps me up in the tip of his trunk, puts me into his mouth and eats me, together with all the leaves and twigs around me*
– *I travel uncomfortably through a twisty, noisy tunnel well over thirty yards long inside the elephant*
– *the elephant ambles along for a mile or more with me inside it, my soft outer flesh being digested all the while*
– *eventually, after some time, the elephant drops me as dung onto a*

jungle track – I love the way an old dropping like this can become decorated with fungi

– quite soon a small hungry rodent spots me and pulls me out of the dung, leaving the clear imprint of where I had been embedded in the dung ball

– the rodent gnaws its way through my very hard shell in order to eat my tasty kernel inside

- *the rodent then abandons me on the track as a mere empty shell with a large hole in me – that's me below.*
- *soon after this a man discovers me alongside the imprint I had left in the dung ball*
- *this man brings me to Singapore and one day flies me to Ireland where he keeps me in his attic*
- *occasionally the man shows me to friends and schoolchildren who are amazed – and relieved to learn that elephant dung is not at all smelly and that some zoos even sell it for enriching garden soil*
- *I am sorry that the elephant ate me mixed up in a bunch of greenery, as I had been hoping to grow into a magnificent forest tree and in due course produce my own fruit*
- *I'm just thinking though – maybe I would not have been a big tree but only a bush that could easily be reached by the trunk of an elephant, since I am pretty sure they cannot climb trees*
- *while making my way through the elephant's tummy I thought I had a good chance of being dropped in a spot where the warm moist jungle soil would allow me to grow, then bud, then flower, then fruit*

– I am annoyed however that the rodent chewed through my protective shell and ate up all my insides, because now I am just a useless empty shell

– but, upon reflection, I am not sad. I am happy that my adventure has given pleasure and interest to the man who found me and to all the people to

whom he has shown me, plus, I hope, all who read about me in his book.

Signed: The Elephant Nut

This apparently childish story carries with it one tiny illustration of the cycle of inter-related plant and animal life going on all round those who dwell in, and those who visit, all the tropical rain forests of the world with their infinitely varied secret treasures. At this point I realise that it is a little hard on elephants just to illustrate their dung without showing wondering readers what the animals themselves look like. Here therefore is a photo of elephants in Thailand, formerly used there for extracting felled timber, but now in a new career waiting to give rides to tourists - definitely an experience to try.

Rather amazingly, one still today sees the occasional elephant being ridden by its mahout along the streets of Bangkok amongst all the rush of modern traffic. My second elephant photo is quite ridiculous when you come to think of it, since elephants, to my certain knowledge, do not use umbrellas and in any case they quite enjoy getting wet.

ETHIOPIAN RIVERS AND DESERTS

A tributary of the
Blue Nile

Awash River

Next is a photo of a very different Ethiopian river with the rather appropriate name Awash. It also rises in the high plateau but in this case its route is eastwards in the direction of the Red Sea, but it never reaches it. In this shot it is seen in spate during the rains, coloured a muddy brown, and heading for oblivion in a vast series of swamps and lakes in the surreal and active volcanic landscape close to the border of Djibouti. There, all that huge volume of water evaporates in the inferno-like heat. It is in that unbelievably hostile landscape (fringing The Great Rift Valley which extends from far down into central Africa via the Red Sea right to the north of Syria), that only in recent years the discovery has been made that Earth's very earliest Man had lived. Our ancestors? What kind of existence can have been eked out by these beings in such a spot?

There are two main rivers which converge to form the River Nile, one of the world's great rivers. One of these is the Blue Nile which emerges from Lake Tana on the great plateau comprising the bulk of Ethiopia. Here is a photo of a small tributary of the Blue Nile not far from Addis Ababa. During the three months of the rainy season vast quantities of topsoil are washed away from the mostly bare plateau. These riches of water and nutrients eventually flow through Egypt, before debouching via the Nile Delta into the Mediterranean. In that warm inland sea, I, and no doubt many readers, will have bathed in water infinitesimally mingled with that ancient land of Ethiopia, or Abyssinia as it was formerly called. Having lived both there and in Lebanon, not far north of the Nile Delta, I like that connection.

Danakil tribesmen in the searing desert scrub,
eastern Ethiopia, 300 miles from Dalol with its
salt deposits, the hottest place on the planet

THE HOLY LAND
Holy to Christian, Moslem and Jew

In the Old City, Jerusalem

A shepherd in the wilderness of Judaea – a landscape known to Jesus
and to countless familiar biblical figures

The Jordan Valley

Bedouin women and their animals in the blinding, stifling, mid-day heat – even the pi-dog lopes listessly behind. The overhead shadows tell the time of day here between the Dead Sea (the lowest point on earth) and Jericho.

ABOVE

Fruit and vegetables for sale in Palestinian old Jerusalem

LEFT

A very special sign indicating sea-level on the road from Jerusalem to Jericho – and my four kids in 1964. In spring this scene would be colourful with wild flowers.

One hundred miles south of the Dead Sea is Aqaba, hemmed in by harsh arid mountains. This is the Transjordan police post in 1949 and the group of people on the left are gathered round a well.

RESCUE BY THE HEJAZ RAILWAY

Back in 1949 I accompanied two Palestinian business colleagues on a visit by 'road' from Amman in Transjordan (now Jordan) to Aqaba on the north-eastern arm of the Red Sea, stopping overnight on our return at isolated Ma'an. There had been much rain in the area and it was still pouring down as we headed northwards. Quite soon it became apparent that we were facing trouble as a number of lorries were stuck fast up to their chassis in mud, and we had well over 100 miles to cover.

We knew that twice weekly a train ran from Ma'an to Amman and that one was due to depart Ma'an that very morning. The question was – could we somehow intercept it and could it accommodate us? So, for a few agonising miles our car slithered and lurched across virtually impassable terrain, with two of us sometimes even having to get out to survey the next few yards ahead – until we spotted the black smoke of the engine far across the flat desert. There then began a Wild West race

to reach a railway halt on our map at a point where there was not even a village marked – could we possibly reach it before the train? Somehow we made it with 90 seconds to spare, so our luck was in. Not only that, but there was a small loading ramp by the track and the train driver was willing to telephone Amman for permission to delay the train. The next problem was that the ramp was at right-angles to the track, so – how to manoeuvre the car onto the single available wagon space on the train? Answer – simple! Shunt the train a bit and get the obliging Arab passengers to lift the car into position. Obvious really! Other railways take note! Success after an hour's hard labour with much shouting and conflicting instructions. Thus we ended our journey in style sitting in the car on the last flat-wagon of the train, watching the desert retreating behind us.

The Hejaz Railway has had a fascinating and chequered history. An attempt by the Ottoman Turks had been made to develop it during the First World War to provide a through connection from Damascus in Syria to Medina, via Transjordan and on to Mecca in what is now Saudi Arabia. However the very stretch on which we had travelled had been frequently attacked by Lawrence of Arabia and his bedouin guerillas, with trains repeatedly being blown up – indeed our train proceeded slowly over many repaired culverts. Ambitious plans are at present afoot by the Jordan Government to upgrade and extend the line to establish a firm rail link through from Damascus to Aqaba, Jordan's only port. Today it is a place of the greatest importance to Jordan – strategically, as the country's only port and as a tourist destination, but at the time of our 1949 visit it was small, remote, sleepy and apparently of little significance. Its setting with palm-fringed beaches below craggy bare mountains is starkly beautiful. The important Israeli town of Eilat, then little more than a desert settlement, lies right next door at the head of the Gulf of Aqaba. While in Aqaba we went out with the local fishermen to catch barracuda off the empty coastline. Truly a place I like to remember just as it was.

Here are three photographs I took of our unusual travel experience.

Dark skies highlight Aya Sofia in Istanbul, Turkey, once the largest cathedral in the world, then a mosque and now a museum. It is one of the finest examples of Byzantine architecture.

A street scene in Calcutta, although the rickshaw is now an outmoded form of transport in the India of today. There is just a hint of the overpopulation facing the world. I know India particularly well having spent all of thirty-six hours there!

RIGHT: A tranquil scene near Abeokuta, a short distance from the frenetic bustle and noise of Lagos, Nigeria

ABOVE: On Victoria Beach, Lagos, Nigeria, fishermen put out to sea in time-honoured fashion.

LEFT: In the Cameron Highlands, Malaysia, ethnic Chinese Malaysians grow vegetables and fruit, which cannot be grown in the hot lowlands, on irrigated steep terracing reminiscent of mainland China.

BELOW: A typical countryside house with an attap (palm) roof in West Malaysia. Being on stilts keeps it cooler, raises it above annual monsoon floods and helps to keep vermin at bay. Similar houses exist all over the Far East.

Many coastal fishing communities Malaysia live such stilted wellings over e sea, where they are ulnerable to storm and sunami. Kids run about oblivious of the risks.

An Indonesian heads towards a small country mosque in Java. The reddish-brown splatter low on the walls bears testimony to the torrential rains on the laterite track.

Ferries ply the river in the blazing noonday sun, Mersing, Kelantan, West Malaysia.

FAR RIGHT: Padi fields in Cambodia produce two rice-crops per year. In the distance a farmer ploughs with a buffalo and welcome rain looms.

RIGHT: Different forms of transport seen from a taxi in Saigon (now Ho Chi Minh City), Vietnam

ABOVE: A fisherman by the Ping River, Chiang Mai, North Thailand

RIGHT: Deftly casting a net into a pond – or into the sea – in Thailand generally brings some reward.

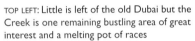

TOP LEFT: Little is left of the old Dubai but the Creek is one remaining bustling area of great interest and a melting pot of races

ABOVE: The Twin Towers of the World Trade Centre, New York, taken in the days of relative innocence pre-9/11. Phyl, a friend and myself marvelled at the panorama from the top.

FAR LEFT: Looking down a colonnade of the magnificent new Grand Mosque, Muscat, Oman, where some shade is found.

LEFT: In New England, USA, many of the rivers are spanned by wooden bridges with the warning 'Bridges freeze before roads'. A skid is just as likely in rain!

The Japanese
Garden in Vancouver   73

I like photographing washing hanging out to dry – so you have been warned! Drying would not take very long in this Andalusian village in Spain.

This early morning view of the Alhambra, Granada, Spain, gives little hint of the Moorish treasures within.

Dramatic plants adapt to this arid spot on the volcanic slopes of Mount Teide, Tenerife.

Just in time for lucky us, thick low clouds and drizzle parted to reveal this magnificent cirque at Gavarnie in the French Pyrenees.

An early mist lies in the valley beyond picturesque Collonge-La Rouge in the Dordogne, France.

ABOVE

Above Grindelwald, Switzerland, hangs the famous north face of the Eiger, with its neighbour, Mönch on its right.

ABOVE RIGHT

A shower in Riva del Garda

Two Danish ladies on a very hot day keeping their nine toddlers happy with ice-cream – ignoring for now the job of dealing with nine sticky faces and ninety sticky fingers – and maybe other problems …

Happy sightseers enjoying brilliant weather in Copenhagen's colourful and lively Nyhavn.

4
Skiing on the road to Damascus

What on earth ......!
My chapter title serves to usher in my love of snow and ice and of the endless photo opportunities they have provided. Unlike Saint Paul I did not have any religious conversion on that famous road. The only conversion I had was from the vertical to the horizontal! This last point says something about my skiing ability which is not, and never was, of the highest order, but I did at least do what the chapter suggests and, apart from the friend with whom I indulged in this escapade in February 1950, I have never met anyone who has done this. Maybe it is one for the *Guinness Book of Records* as it is unlikely to be repeated, since, sixty years on, traffic on that famous road would make such a caper suicidal.

This is Damascus, Syria, as you are not likely to have seen it.

There is no photograph to prove that I did it but the above photo was taken in Damascus that morning from the house in which I was staying for the weekend. I am sure it is a scene far from your mental image of Damascus, the oldest continuously inhabited city on earth. I can only ask you to believe me – indeed is it not surely almost too bizarre an antic to have invented? We had the twisting road entirely to ourselves as it had been blocked by drifts higher up, so we swooped round bends on hired skis between snowy crests such as that in the photo. Further, I even have a letter I wrote home to my parents in Belfast dating this escapade precisely.

I paid many business trips to Damascus from Beirut where I was living from 1948 to 1952 and during that period I experienced every winter an astonishing amount of snow in the mountains with many road travel disruptions.

Plodding on near the summit of the road between Beirut and Damascus.

Ski climb, Laqlooq

Snow and sky – favourite ski slopes above Beirut to which, and other spots, I had many happy outings with the local sports club. Beirut was then (1948–52) one of the best of overseas postings and it was said that one could ski and sea-bathe within the same hour. I proved it.

Snowed in at the Cedars of Lebanon

On one never-to-be-forgotten occasion in 1949 I was snowed up at the Cedars of Lebanon, of several biblical mentions, for a whole week before being able to escape, partly on ski, to a village below the snow-line. Our plight (?) had been reported in the local papers and we were welcomed back to work by colleagues with what can only be described as envy and some questions as to why we had not managed to escape earlier. We couldn't. Truly. In Psalm 29 verse 9 reads 'the voice of the Lord breaks the cedars of Lebanon' – I can testify to having seen massive cedars broken in that storm.

Just think, no two identical snowflakes have ever been discovered. Of all the miracles of nature I find this one of the most astounding, when one considers the unimaginable numbers that have been formed and made their way to earth over countless millennia. We are talking here of some number with so many noughts that it is too difficult for the mind to grasp, trillions, zillions even. Billions would be a mere nothing. And yet just occasionally, given exactly the right atmospheric conditions, one separate ice crystal will drift gently down and will alight on say a dark sleeve. This provides an opportunity to examine and marvel at its unique six-sided crystalline structure through a magnifying glass. Snowflakes comprise clumps of such ice crystals formed under sets of complicated conditions. Snow either evaporates, melts or freezes and becomes ice (useful for cooling drinks)

The cedars in spring

and whichever of these occurs it all finishes as the moisture in clouds which in time deposit on us more snow or hail or rain.

The significance of ice, much of it being compacted snow, is being brought home to us through the reporting of dramatic occurrences like vast chunks of the Antarctic ice shelf breaking away into melting floating islands the size of some countries, and by the shrinking of glaciers across the planet. These and other equally visible and measurable events are the main factors leading to the likelihood of sea levels rising, with catastrophic consequences. The significance of these ice-events can scarcely be overstated, whether they be brought about by periodic natural fluctuations or by the activities of mankind or a combination of these. They cannot be ignored.

But my interest in these pages is not so much in the power of ice to affect our climate, our weather and hence the lives of everyone, everywhere and every day. My interest lies in the beauty, variety and intricacy of ice and snow – and not least the infinite scope it offers photographers, even without visiting the North Pole or the South Pole.

And what about the sport it provides? Skating, skiing and the rest, preceded by childhood fun like sledging, snowballing and so on, always worth the agony of thawing out frozen fingers and toes, followed by a hot drink to restore life. There is nothing like it. I hope you will agree with me when you look at the photographs that follow and maybe accept that there is much more to ice and snow than winter chill and inconvenience. But treat it with respect – whatever age you may be! You may well have photos that excited you but here are a few that excited me, not least the close-ups.

After explaining my unlikely chapter title, I now move on from the joys of winter in Syria and Lebanon to a few favourite photos rather closer to home.

The last remaining cedars
in deep winter

ABOVE

Breithorn straddles Switzerland and Italy. The lone, tiny figure (bottom centre) obligingly came into my viewfinder to indicate scale. He and I are both enthralled at the view before us from our very different perspectives.

ABOVE RIGHT

Soaring above the ice formations en route to Titlis in central Switzerland

The Matterhorn is here seen across a lake above Zermatt, one of the world's most dramatic peaks, which is familiar as Alpen at the breakfast table in many homes.

FAR LEFT

Overlooking a lake near Stavanger, Norway

LEFT

This rime-covered stone stands near the summit of Scafell Pike, England's highest mountain.

ABOVE: a Thames barge at Teddington laden with snow

LEFT: Phyl and icicles above Dirdal Fjord, Rogaland, Norway – which reminds me that in the late 1950s I was Hon. Norwegian Vice-Consul in Penang, Malaysia (never having been to Norway at that point!). Not too onerous a post, mainly involving social representation.

RIGHT

Phyl is spellbound here early one morning by the Lagan on the southern outskirts of Belfast.

BELOW

On a bitter winter's day by St Malachy's church in Belfast. This area has since been wonderfully redeveloped.

RIGHT

The old Quoile bridge near Downpatrick, long since bypassed by the main road to Belfast

FAR RIGHT

Hardy weather in the Mournes and a shepherding job for husband and wife

Slemish, a volcanic plug sits conspicuously in mid-Antrim.

A falling tide in Strangford Bay after a heavy night frost produces this strange effect.

LEFT

Above Magilligan in Co. Derry is Gortmore viewpoint looking towards Binevenagh and Lough Foyle.

FAR LEFT CENTRE

The flat-topped ridge of Lurigethan sits alongside Glenariff (left) and Glenballyemon, Co. Antrim. Snow remains longest on north-facing slopes.

FAR LEFT BOTTOM

A smattering of snow by the edge of Fair Head looking towards Rathlin.

THERE IS NO END TO
SUCH WONDERS

5

Elemental forces and climate

In this chapter we consider those elemental forces that have helped to form the Earth and in particular those whose effects we can actually see and can hence be at least partially understood by laymen like me. We glimpse evidence of some of the forces that have helped to shape the world as we know it including our own islands – earthquakes, volcanoes, winds, waves, rain, snow, ice, heat, erosion and decay. I attempt to link these forces to our daily lives in Britain and Ireland, and to the lives of peoples who inhabit very different landscapes and climates elsewhere.

The restless waves of the Atlantic on a calm day –
Slea Head, Co. Kerry

A ferocious monsoon storm from the Gulf of Thailand hits Prachuab Khiri Khan.

A sea wall half a mile from my house takes a battering. The navigation marker visible in the distance has since been demolished by the waves.

There are amongst us adventure seekers and scientists who do such things as pursue tornadoes either for the thrill of the chase or for scientific research. There are others who engage in equally dangerous and dramatic activities, such as volcanologists, potholers, deep sea divers, mountaineers, arctic explorers and the like. Not only do these pursuits tax a person's physical and mental strength and endurance but they must be thrilling. Many of them have become increasingly essential in the pursuit of science for mankind. However I do not plan to copy them. Instead, I draw on my more limited experiences of elemental forces and on my own observations of some of their climatic and other effects. So, along the way I share some of my relatively tame exploits.

Niagara Falls is one of the world's most celebrated waterfalls, part of it in the US and part in Canada (mistily in the distance here). A ride on the 'Maid of the Mist' right into the boiling cauldron below the falls is an experience not to be missed – but do choose a position on the vessel where you and your camera will not be drenched!

Arabian sand dunes on the move are constantly sculpted by the wind. What can have made the footprints diagonally across the foreground?

Jeita Grotto, a short distance north of Beirut, Lebanon, was little known in 1950 when five of us lads, wearing headlamps, paddled and scrambled for over half a mile into it with small rubber dinghies. If ever beauty and mystery were indescribable it must surely be here, where God was the sculptor, with limestone, water and chemical reactions the only mediums, producing a 3-dimensional result in many hues and intricacy simply beggaring description. This photograph was only achieved thanks to one of the others concealing himself behind a huge stalagmite (or maybe a stalagtite linking cave ceiling to cave floor) where he burned a length of magnesium ribbon – after a struggle with damp matches. Our Lebanese leader, Lionel, went on to form the first local speleological group and the caves are today a world renowned tourist attraction, with photography not permittted.

Near the summit of the Jungfrau, Switzerland, where one feels that weather is truly born. I cannot claim to have climbed to this point; there is a dramatic mountain railway and at the top one can wander through ice tunnels cut into the glacier, admiring ice sculptures.

Like all who have lived for years in the tropics, I have experienced many terrifying thunderstorms and have had close shaves with lightning. On one day in December 1971 in Singapore 17.3 inches of rain fell over a 30 hour period (equivalent to over 6 months' rain in Strangford) accompanied by relentless thunder and lightning. Many streets in the city became rivers but such was the efficiency of the monsoon drains for coping with periodic lesser deluges that there was little sign of it the next day. Incredibly though, I have been (very slightly) touched by lightning – I hesitate to use the word struck – while washing lettuce at the sink in our own kitchen in Strangford, while less than a mile away at that time a mini-tornado hit. Clearly my time had not yet come but the burglar alarm was fried. Beware of washing lettuce!

In Tollymore Park, Co. Down, stands this telling exploded remains of a sequoia tree (giant redwood) struck by lightning in 1988. A witness who was alarmingly close tells of the debris being scattered far and wide, with the adjacent ground being furrowed by the blast, an effect I have observed in the tropics. Ros enjoyed indicating scale!

Everyone in the British Isles has to cope with most of the extremes of our weather occasionally – colossal rains, gales up to hurricane force and the resultant mountainous seas around our coasts. I have known spells of bitter cold and great snows, including the notorious early 1947 during the post-war austerities. Once too, thanks to the antics of other motorists (yes!) I even had to abandon my car on the Irish border between Dublin and Belfast. However most of my snow experiences have been in the Middle East, as you will have read in Chapter 4. But, like all my readers, thank goodness I managed to avoid the last Ice Age! This covered much of the British Isles, yet I see around me every day those small gently rounded hills called drumlins which are the evidence of the retreating ice a mere 14000 years ago. These are a notable feature of the landscape of much of County Down and other parts of Ireland; little lakes and swamps, each one a mini-wildlife haven, often lie between these drumlins.

Here where the River Quoile enters Strangford Lough are little islands, some of the many drowned drumlins forming gentle patterns in the sea, visible to varying degrees according to the state of the tide. The land all round the lough is dotted with drumlins.

The dark basaltic cliffs of the Giant's Causeway in Co. Antrim are here dusted with snow. In this forbidding setting the 'Gerona' of the Spanish Armada was wrecked in a fierce storm in 1588, with heavy loss of life. Its fabulous treasures, only recovered by divers in 1967, are on display at the Ulster Museum in Belfast.

Volcanoes have been features of the landscape of Earth since Creation. In my travels I have seen the perils that people are taking every day by farming the rich soil that lies around the slopes of volcanoes that will one day erupt again. We run no such obvious risks in the British Isles, for the volcanic activity that did take place here is so far in the distant past that the dangers are probably insignificant in the extreme. However some of the clearest dramatic evidence of past volcanic upheavals to be seen anywhere is to be found in County Antrim. Here dark lava swept over the original white limestone, burying much of it and its fossils laid down when seas covered the area. Where the lava cooled into amazing basaltic columnar rock formations we now have Northern Ireland's renowned Giant's Causeway, a UNESCO World Heritage Site, almost wholly owned by the National Trust. This same rock formation also appears across the North Channel on the island of Staffa in Scotland. My photos show examples of County Antrim's violent geological story.

This story is apparent at Garron Point on the thrillingly beautiful Antrim Coast Road.

Baalbek in Lebanon's Beqaa Valley has suffered from the ravages of time including wars and earthquakes but its Roman ruins still tell much about its vanished splendours.

As for earthquakes, when I lived in earthquake-prone zones in several countries for many years, I never noticed a single tremor. Yet here in County Down I have felt and heard in recent years two small quakes, one with its epicentre in north Wales some 130 miles away and the other in Lincolnshire at twice that distance. Astonishingly, the first of these events resulted in the collapse of walls and a roof inside a semi-derelict warehouse at Strangford Harbour.

Many parts of the world expect to suffer earthquakes, even as close as Mediterranean countries. Some quakes result in massive destruction, huge loss of life and resettlement of vast numbers of people. The effects can be mitigated by earthquake drills, by appropriate architectural design, and by the provision of shelters. Meanwhile strenuous efforts continue towards predicting where and when earthquakes might occur along or close to known fault lines like the San Andreas fault in California. However, so far, the most reliable indicator of something abnormal about to occur seems to be animal behaviour, such as unaccountable restiveness. Mankind has much to learn in this field.

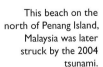

Snakes have apparently been successfully used in experiments to predict earthquakes, though not this particular species. This is a Paradise Green Tree Snake in a Malaysian forest, one of several species of so-called flying snakes – it does not fly but rather it glides by extending a narrow fold of skin down each side of its body which, when extended, enables it to descend from a higher tree branch to a lower one, twisting its body as it would were it moving on the ground. It is a particularly beautiful and harmless snake which I have seen in action several times.

Tsunamis are caused by undersea earthquakes and the catastrophic one in December 2004 off the north-west coast of Sumatra in Indonesia, affecting vast areas around the rim of the Indian Ocean, even extending to Africa, with appalling devastation and casualties, was the result of a sudden movement between the sea floor's tectonic plates forming the earth's crust. The word tsunami originated in Japan where they are not uncommon, but they can occur in many coastal parts of the world, with clear evidence of past tsunamis being found in some parts of Britain, notably around the Bristol Channel. News has just broken of a huge earthquake hitting Padang further south on the Sumatran coast.

This beach on the north of Penang Island, Malaysia was later struck by the 2004 tsunami.

Only 200 miles inland from the epicentre of that terrible event off Sumatra lies Lake Toba. That huge lake, over 50 miles long by 15 miles wide, lies in the caldera formed by a supervolcano which erupted 74000 years ago, Earth's largest recorded eruption. Much of the fertile mountainous land around it is inhabited by the Batak tribe, originally Neolithic mountain people from north Thailand and Burma, who practise a blend of Christianity and animism. There is certainly an atmosphere of mystery pervading this remote and incredibly beautiful area, which only by a whisker avoided being the spot from which all life was snuffed out, either by the various effects of the unimaginably huge explosion or by the subsequent years of 'volcanic winter' and ice age that followed it. I was privileged to visit the area for a few days in 1970.

There is clear indication here of the ancient culture of the Bataks on Samosir island in the vastness of Lake Toba.

Mount Teide, set in a Spanish National Park filled with superlatives, dominates the island of Tenerife in the Canaries. It is 12,188 feet high, the highest mountain in Spain, and is considered one of the twenty potentially most dangerous volcanoes in the world; it last erupted in 1909. Reckoning its total height from the adjacent sea bed makes it the world's third highest volcano after Hawaii.

A number of hotspots on earth which could explode with the force of a supervolcano have been identified, and the one thought to be in the most imminent risk of erupting is Yellowstone in Wyoming State in the US, though monitoring of it has found no recent significant sinister activity. If, or rather when, this occurs the dramatic effects are likely to be felt not only in North America but across the globe. Other cataclysmic events looming include possible asteroid strikes which could be of unknown size and could affect anywhere. Another major natural occurrence could be the collapse into the North Atlantic of an almost sheer mountain on La Palma Island in the Canaries, triggered by any nearby earthquake. The resultant tsunami could affect vast coastal areas of Africa, NW Europe and the east coast of America. Any one of these occurrences could hugely affect the entire world climate. But, just as a rainy day might dawn when you least want it, worrying won't help!

Mount Hood, at 11,000 feet the highest peak in Oregon, USA is a mere 60 miles from Mount St. Helens. I wish I had taken a pre-eruption photo of the latter instead, but I was sitting on the wrong side of the aircraft. Anyway who could have known about the looming eruption a few years later?

Relatively small recent, but locally hugely significant, convulsions within the earth have included: the eruption of Mt. St. Helens in Washington State (a mere 600 miles from Yellowstone) in 1980; the birth from the sea off SE Iceland of Surtsey Island in the Westmann Islands in 1965, when the ocean boiled as if it were the beginnings of time; many other huge eruptions in South and Central America, the Mediterranean, the Far East and Kamchatka in eastern Siberia. As for Iceland's surface – much of it is like a barely set jelly shaken by daily small tremors. Even as I write an under-sea volcano has erupted (caught magnificently on film) and formed a pumice island close to the Pacific island of Tonga with an accompanying large earthquake. As we go to press that same geologically unstable region around Tonga and Samoa has been devastated by tsunamis and quakes.

However probably the most dramatic sight ever recorded by mariners, fishermen and watchers on land was the 1883 explosion and total disappearance of the island of Krakatoa between Java and Sumatra in Indonesia. For years the dust and ash in the atmosphere from this event produced dramatic sunrise and sunset effects around the globe. This eruption has been followed by the appearance from beneath the sea nearby of the much smaller Anak Krakatoa (meaning son of Krakatoa) which already shows signs of not lasting for ever. Nothing does. If you want proof, look now at the photo below.

While visiting Bandung in Java, Indonesia, Phyl and I went with friends into the crater of this volcano, Pangkuban Perahu, where the smell of sulphur and the brooding atmosphere were powerful. I was not surprised to hear of its eruption some years later. Friend and colleague Peter seems to be delivering a lecture!

Erosion of the stonework and rot in the wooden door tell of the processes of decay at work here above Lake Garda in Italy in a partially restored medieval village.

In Chiang Mai in the slightly cooler North Thailand hill country, oriental umbrellas made of oiled paper dry in the sun before a design is applied.

Earth is indeed dynamic; in other words it is still in the process of being moulded, as we have seen, so the human race can count itself lucky to have made it through, relatively unscathed, until now. An umbrella is fine to protect you against rain and drizzle but useless against volcanic ash! Do not therefore bother laying in emergency umbrellas for the family after reading this. Just enjoy the present and its daily dose of weather, whether or not it calls for an umbrella. Usually not.

A young camel grazes near Aden where no other animal would find anything tempting.

Belfast shoppers sport umbrellas on a nasty drizzly day in Donegall Place, with its blend of old and modern facades. The dome of the fine City Hall is in the background.

Leave your umbrella behind if you visit Aden. However almost all deserts do, just occasionally, have rain and it can be cataclysmic and change the face of the landscape, so here is a short traveller's tale. When I lived briefly in Aden in the mid-1950s, before it became absorbed in Yemen, one day there was a sudden downpour and all the drivers who had long since removed their wipers could hardly see to drive through the dust-turned-to-mud on their windscreens. This photo shows how the land has been shaped by volcanic activity and erosion.

Before an effective tidal barrage was built in 1956 small ships once tied up in Downpatrick town centre, but it was often flooded when high spring tides from Strangford Lough coincided with floods from the River Quoile in spate. The area above the barrage was left to regenerate naturally and it is now a popular nature reserve and a haven for water birds and many other forms of wildlife. Here is a sunset over floodwaters at Jane's Shore.

This is Ca' d'Oro on the Grand Canal, Venice where the problem is that the sheer weight of ancient buildings constructed on piles in the mud of the lagoon bed is causing them to sink, exacerbated by the wash of boat traffic. Then at times of extra high tides, pushed up the Adriatic Sea by storms, the water level overtops the defences and flooding often occurs. The threat posed by climate change will mean ever higher tides, thus endangering the unique heritage of this island city. Work is therefore in progress to increase the height of flood defences, while some old sinking buildings are being underpinned.

Other parts of the world have to cope with more water that they want, as the above images show. Getting the balance right is the difficulty and without dams, reservoirs, levees and the like water would be even more of a problem than it can be for many. Yet, in moderation it is a blessing and without it where would we be? And how will many countries, including some areas of the British Isles, cope with impending rising sea levels expected before the end of this century? Apocalypse for some?

Now follow more examples of the elemental forces which have played their part – and still do today – in helping to make us all what we are.

Solomon's Pools near Bethlehem, going back thousands of years and still in use in the 1940s when I was there.

A distinctly less ancient reservoir, Ben Crom, above the Silent Valley in the Mournes. Bus at lower right gives an idea of scale.

ICE, WATER AND GLACIATION

RIGHT

The thunderous roar, earthy smell, wafting spray and above all the endless onrush of water were dizzying and I was oblivious of the crowds around me as I absorbed the awe-inspiring spectacle of the Canadian Niagara Falls.

BELOW LEFT

Reagh and Mahee Islands (foreground and left) and all this region of Strangford Lough in Co. Down are products of the last Ice-Age which left a legacy of many islands and small rounded hills. The circular stonework on Mahee is the remains of the ancient Nendrum monastery and stump of a round tower.

BELOW RIGHT

Another impressive example of glaciation is Ordesa National Park in the Spanish Pyrenees

Jungfrau from Interlaken, Switzerland, spotlit by the last rays of the sun below a gibbous moon.

This is Afqa cave, Lebanon, from which water flows, icy cold and refreshing in summer

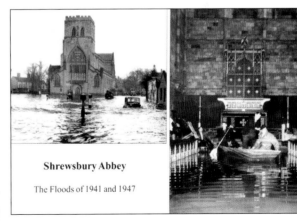

Shrewsbury Abbey

The Floods of 1941 and 1947

The River Severn almost encircles Shrewsbury so it suffers from frequent floods. This is a postcard from Shrewsbury Abbey (with kind permission) that tells the story better than any words.

LEFT: Water issuing from Gorner Glacier's snout in Switzerland, with dirty ice and moraine above. Phyl standing at upper left shows the scale.

THUNDER
& FIRE

Blacksmith and apprentice put fire to good use at an agricultural fair near Saintfield.

Fire can consume all in its path and smoke can choke and pollute. Arsonists or human thoughtlessness all too often disastrously perform nature's more limited essential work of fire.

The black cloud here, seen from Copenhagen Harbour, caused floods in some areas but not a drop of rain fell on our boat, its roof acting as a mirror in this shot – with bottle top in foreground.

For much of the year the daily heat in Malaysia sets off big thunderstorms – this is one retreating in the evening beyond Mersing in Kelantan.

A violent thunderstorm with heavy hail developed from this menacing sky near Downpatrick.

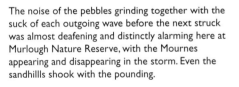

The bride at Down Cathedral's exposed entrance door faces the same problem as Tomás.

The noise of the pebbles grinding together with the suck of each outgoing wave before the next struck was almost deafening and distinctly alarming here at Murlough Nature Reserve, with the Mournes appearing and disappearing in the storm. Even the sandhillls shook with the pounding.

TOP RIGHT: The gales howl on the Blasket Islands, Co. Kerry, and this statue of island author Tomás Ó Criomthain at nearby Blasket Centre on the mainland says it all.

RIGHT: Trees, especially when in full leaf, are vulnerable to gales inland, but most trees in coastal areas have grown into a more resilient shape sculpted by the local prevailing wind.

The cliffs near Mount Brandon in Co. Kerry can cope with Atlantic waves.

A Mediterranean storm can blow up quite suddenly – Kyrenia, North Cyprus

VOLCANOES & QUAKES

RIGHT: The beautiful, lush, green island of Java in Indonesia has its location, on the boundary between two of the earth's tectonic plates, to thank for its fertility. Its dense population lives at constant risk from volcanic eruptions and earthquakes, but this productive land delivers its bounty, so people stay.

FAR RIGHT: A corner of Lake Toba in N. Sumatra where the eruption of 74,000 years ago almost exterminated all forms of life right across the globe.

LEFT: Rome has experienced many earthquakes. The Forum here has been pillaged too for stone building materials.

BELOW: Above Cushendall on the Antrim Coast Road is Tieveragh, an eroded cone of a small volcano.

ABOVE
A dark, grey day at Piha beach in North Island, New Zealand, with its volcanic black sand

RIGHT
Carrick-a-Rede island, linked to the mainland by rope bridge, is part of an ancient volcano

FAR LEFT

After camping near Lake Shala (here) in Ethiopia I enjoyed the experience of shaving with nature's own hot water while watching hippos far out in this volcanic lake.

LEFT

Close by Mount Teide in Tenerife is this volcanic valley, a dust devil moving across its floor

Geothermal energy is the thing in Iceland. Here in a desolate spot are geysers near Reykjavik.

EROSION & DECAY

RIGHT

RIGHT

Granite tors on Slieve Bignian in the Mournes, gradually eroding by the action of rain, frost and wind.

BELOW

The cliffs of Benbulbin in Co. Sligo clearly show erosion by heavy rains.

BELOW RIGHT

Ightham Moate in Kent, a mediaeval property owned by the National Trust, needs constant repair, as does any man-made structure, however modest it may be in comparison.

The Chasms near the Calf of Man occasionally tumble away in vast chunks.

TOP

Exposed ground on the jungle floor gets washed away by torrential rains, leaving these small 'pillars', each protected by a small leaf or twig, while the soil is washed into streams, then rivers and ultimately the sea.

ABOVE CENTRE

The crumbling basaltic cliffs at Downhill, Co. Derry, have dropped boulders occasionally onto road and rail, resulting in accidents, so protective netting has been fitted in danger spots.

LEFT

A Samson post from an old shipwreck, now part of a farmer's fence, but it must ultimately rot away.

6

Energy from the sun

East and West, our sun ushers in another day

Over the Irish Sea

Over the Gulf of Thailand

Our Earth moves round the sun and from it comes all life and not least all forms of energy, even indirectly nuclear energy since it is the fruit of human scientific advances. One consequence of this is the debate about fossil fuel versus nuclear power, combined with the accent on renewable energy.

Next, it is not, I believe, trite to say this: we are all in a sense creatures of the sun. Without it, nothing – no light, no heat, no colour, no weather and so no book about weather. No plant life. And of course no us. In this this chapter I have interspersed through the text spreads of photographs divided into topics.

Let us now look at the sun sparkling through this prism from Prague hanging by my skylight bringing the heat, light and colour we all accept as normal. In the dazzling facets of a prism we see a hint of the energy on which everything depends and which we have come to take for granted.

This chapter is the deadly earnest part of this book through the eyes of a layman who keeps himself reasonably informed of the escalating climate change issue and its global consequences. I have touched on this earlier but enlarge on it now. I accept that this is a developing story and that it could in part be out of date even before you read it, but it is an attempt to set out some of the issues at the time of going to press. You might well feel you have heard all my points before and so feel like 'switching off'. You may therefore just wish to skim through these next paragraphs, but I hope you will at the very least enjoy and mull over my photographs, each of which has a point to make.

A magnificent performer at a Thai temple crows defiantly: Wake up! This could be interpreted as a warning about climate change.

As a result of both man-made CO_2 (carbon dioxide) emissions and cyclical climatic upheavals, both Arctic and Antarctic ice is now melting at a much greater rate than in recent past times. This has been scientifically recorded backed by visual evidence. Relatively few people visit or inhabit these desolate regions and it is difficult for the average person, myself included, to comprehend the sheer volume of ice locked up in the polar ice caps. As it melts – at an accelerating rate – sea levels across the globe are inevitably rising with potentially devastating consequences, especially for low-lying areas. Let us now look nearer home at an Atlantic current of which most of us are at least vaguely aware.

The Gulf Stream, an ocean current which originates in the Gulf of Mexico, flows north-eastwards off the US coast before turning eastwards off the Grand Banks near Newfoundland. It then broadens and forms the slower-moving North Atlantic Current whose benign warm waters bathe most of the shores of Western Europe, keeping its climate relatively equable, neither too hot nor too cold. It has been suggested, however, that the increased melting of the Arctic ice-cap, apparently driven by global warming, could switch off the flow of the warm water to Western Europe by restricting the formation and circulation of the deep waters of the oceans. This seems to have happened –

Equally symbolic is the march of time spelled out by this ancient sundial on the Old Market House in historic Shrewsbury.

A sure sign of hope in the world – if we act now.

and happened quickly – during the past 10,000 years or so. If that occurred now, Britain and Ireland would be in for an abrupt and severe shock,

SOME ENERGY SOURCES

FAR RIGHT

Firewood near
Castlewellan

RIGHT

South-facing solar panel
for heating water,
with photovoltaic cell
powering pump

ABOVE: Belfast Corporation Gas Works – as it used to be. This view is now completely different.

LEFT: a surviving working windmill in Lincolnshire

Sellafield, Cumbria

experiencing the kind of bitingly cold winters of Labrador in Eastern Canada – a bleak climate scenario indeed. More recent thinking suggests that the changes may be less severe but, as always with climate, who knows what changes are in store?

On a more everyday scale, much the same doubts apply to our daily weather forecasts in which, amongst the huge number of variable factors constantly being monitored by Meteorological Offices, a mere one degree temperature difference or a slight shift in wind direction can, for example, mean either snow or rain falling following a forecast predicting the opposite of what things turn out to be. Many weather-sensitive economic and other decisions can depend on the accuracy of forecasts, not merely whether ice cream manufacturers should step up their production rates in anticipation of a heat wave. It is simply not possible for forecasts to be 100% correct, and certainly not on a localised basis where topography and other factors can significantly influence local daily weather. Is it not cloud cuckoo land to imagine that pinpoint forecasting accuracy could ever be achieved? A hefty downpour could be ruinous to your plans but leave your friends a few miles away – or even closer – basking in warm sunshine, asking what all the fuss is about when you complain about the rotten summer weather.

Setting aside a possible Atlantic deep freeze scenario, majority scientific opinion expects Western Europe to be affected by temperature rise in the same way as most of the rest of the world, leading to ever more extreme weather events like floods, droughts, storms and brutal heat. Low-lying

Beneath these snowy mountain ridges and valleys in Iran lies a wealth of oil.

LEFT

Natural gas platform, Liverpool Bay

FAR LEFT

Wind farm, Liverpool Bay

MORE ENERGY SOURCES

SeaGen is the name of the world's first commercial tidal flow electricity generator. Since Spring 2009 it has been delivering 1.2 megawatts direct into the adjacent grid from the narrows between Strangford and Portaferry in County Down, Northern Ireland. The powerful and reliable marine tidal current regularly attains up to 8 knots with the twice daily tides. As a prototype it has attracted worldwide interest.

LEFT

'Rambiz', one of the world's largest crane barges, placing SeaGen in position on the seabed.

BELOW FROM LEFT

Work in progress to commission SeaGen in mid-stream, seen from Windmill Hill, Portaferry; SeaGen in position with turbine blades raised – figure in door indicates scale; the fast tidal flow surges round SeaGen in action, following exhaustive successful environmental impact studies, which continue.

RIGHT

Ironbridge coal-fired power station in Shropshire

FAR RIGHT

Loch Cloy hydro-electric power station on Loch Lomond sits below Ben Voirlich.

In 1951, on Achill Island, Co. Mayo, turf (peat) from the local bogs was the main source of energy.

Hama, Syria, where the Romans harnessed the energy of the River Orontes to pump water.

islands and parts of many countries may be inundated by rising sea levels. Other places may be rendered uninhabitable by desertification and heat. Fresh water, essential to all life, will be the most sought after commodity. Food shortages and imbalances will worsen, especially amongst today's most needy. The consequences have the potential to include mass starvation, disease, wars and massive population movements.

The implications of all this are of staggering complexity and can only be tackled with full governmental international collaboration. Countries are ill-prepared (some even unwilling), and are maybe too late in the day anyway, to cope with the problems effectively in time to avert catastrophes of monumental proportions. However the air of pessimism, even despair in many minds, has been lightened by the positive approaches taken by Barak Obama to environmental issues so soon after his taking up office as US President in January 2009.

Whilst at last there seems to be some light at the end of the tunnel, this does not in any way lessen the imperative for whole populations to make at least some life-style changes, targeting energy efficiency and involving some measure of sacrifice; this is a concept hard to grasp and even harder to implement. It is too painful and its convolutions are hugely difficult to put across effectively to the world's 6.7 billion (6,700,000,000) inhabitants – escalating alarmingly in numbers.

Meanwhile, partly as a result of wastage and of the consumerism of unthinking luxuries associated with Western society, Earth's finite natural resources are being used up at a startling rate. This is all happening in a world that is increasingly becoming too full of people to sustain the accepted Western standard of

YET MORE ENERGY SOURCES

Annalong corn mill powered by a water wheel

The elegance of the age of sail

An old shot of the River Shannon at Limerick, with inset of the first Irish pictorial stamp of 1930 depicting the Ardnacrusha hydro-electric scheme a few miles upstream.

There is no lack of breeze for drying the washing on Tory Island – but clothes pegs need to be extra firm to prevent the precious garments from ending up in the Atlantic. No tumble dryer needed here.

TRANSPORT BY FOSSIL FUEL

Irish Lights vessel, Granuaile, enters Strangford Lough

living, regarded by so many as both the norm and their right. In recent years this 'Western' standard has, not surprisingly, been seen as the way forward for an increasing number of countries not geographically in the West – they naturally feel it is their turn. At the same time poverty, deprivation, hunger and avoidable ill health continue and even worsen, a blight and a scar on the consciences of civilised people. As ever too, the sickening squandering of human and natural wealth on wars and lesser conflicts continues – a shocking reproach to mankind, all the while nuclear weapon proliferation casts a shadow of unspeakably horrifying possible consequences.

Pollution of land, fresh waters and seas by countries and by shipping, combined with over-fishing and other wasteful fishing practices are problems that go hand in hand with the overall environmental scene. Alarmingly bleak forecasts have been made about the overall health of seas and oceans following years that have included bewildering national and international fishing regulations. I quote only one classic example – the wiping out of cod from the Grand Banks off Newfoundland, once probably one of the most prolific fishing grounds in the world. Now consider today's price of a piece of cod – if you can find it. There have however been successes, with some fish stocks staging recovery, so all is not yet lost. The condition of the sea matters hugely – after all it surrounds many of us and it covers some 70% of the planet's surface. Its food potential and its ability to help combat climate change have yet to be fully realised, but scientists are hard at work on this.

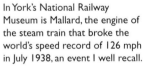

In York's National Railway Museum is Mallard, the engine of the steam train that broke the world's speed record of 126 mph in July 1938, an event I well recall.

A well-laden tram in Beirut, 1948

Diesel railcar, 1955, between Addis Ababa, Ethiopia's capital and independent Djibouti on the Gulf of Aden

On the east coast main line in England this is today's train doing roughly the same speed on the very stretch of line which witnessed that record over seventy years earlier.

ABOVE: a family drops in for lunch at Daft Eddy's by Strangford Lough.

LEFT: a road tanker on a river crossing in Trengganu, Malaysia

ABOVE: a hand-operated petrol pump near Jerusalem, c. 1949

ABOVE LEFT: a 1950 shot of an island ferry near Istanbul, Turkey

LEFT: the present Belfast to Birkenhead ferry berthed below Cave Hill, Belfast

All the while the effects of climate change on plant and animal life worldwide are increasingly being recorded not only in the oceans but on land and in the air. Further, the introduction of alien species, whether accidentally or deliberately, is all too often posing dire threats to native species. In the past two decades I have even recorded my own local evidence of clear changes in the natural world around my own close environs of garden, shore and countryside. For example new birds have arrived (I welcome the little egret) and old favourites have all but disappeared (I do miss the cuckoo) while daffodils bloom a month earlier than they did twenty-five years ago.

One of the most shocking trends in recent years is the massive destruction of tropical rainforests mostly in the Amazon, West Africa and SE Asia, notably in Borneo. This annihilation is either for timber extraction, much of it illegal, or to provide land for growing crops for food and fuel for the world's peoples, many having expectations of rising living standards. Further, this devastation brings with it huge uncontrollable fires and serious regional smoke pollution. Primeval jungle never reverts to its original pristine state, hence at one blow, both biodiversity and one of the most effective 'carbon sinks' are wiped out. Eventually however in the heat and humidity of the tropics dense secondary jungle will grow and will have some lesser carbon sink value, but the virgin forest giants and all their plant and animal biodiversity will have simply become history. This destruction still goes on even after years of awareness of its impact, usually with little regard to the effect it can have on the traditional lives of indigenous tribes.

Scientists of all disciplines and governments now broadly concur that immediate action is essential, though not surprisingly to varying degrees and with equally varying opinions, as to where the emphasis should lie. Nature, combined with scientific research, is clearly telling us with increasing urgency things we can no longer afford to ignore. If ever there was a time for truly radical thinking it is now. Geothermal energy, for example, seems to be one inexhaustible line demanding further research, but there are many other lines of scientific development. Some may be feasible but immensely costly, yet others are almost in the realms of fantasy, some almost laughable even in their apparent simplicity. Yet all – and not least vehicle efficiency – demand their slot of attention leading to decisions with time-scale and feasibility labels attached. Human ingenuity is being tested to the ultimate.

Refuelling from a 4-gallon tin, Ras-al-Ayn, Syria (1949)

A cycle lane separates a Copenhagen bus from the footpath.

MORE TRANSPORT BY FOSSIL FUEL

A gas-guzzler in Dragør, Denmark

1937 Wolseley on my first trip round Ireland in 1951 – the first car I owned for just four months on leave from abroad.

Undeniably an 'oversize load'.

We were driving along at 50 mph admiring the beautiful fall colours in New England, when I was flagged down by a police marshal. My whole guilty past rose up before me as I knew the speed limit there was 45 mph. Quaking somewhat, I rolled down the window and he said in a not-unfriendly tone: 'If I were you buddy, I'd slow down a bit as there's a horse coming along the road.' At least that's what I thought he said but Phyl was sure he had said hearse not horse. What we actually encountered at the next bend was neither horse nor hearse but a house! House moving can mean literally this in the USA. We were lucky that the two-story wooden house, which had been painstakingly sawn in half for the removal, leaving a cuckoo clock still hanging incongruously on one wall, was about to be positioned nearby. So we were able to observe the whole well-rehearsed procedure, up to the point where we were offered a glass of champagne to mark a job well done. Just as those folks were friendly, this has since struck me as being environmentaly friendly too.

It takes no ingenuity, however, to plant trees in empty corners or on boundaries, especially in the countryside – for carbon capture, for beauty and for benefiting wildlife. At the same time farmers could be encouraged to spare sturdy saplings when hedge-trimming. All this is apparently simple, but demanding a more pro-active governmental attitude.

Public attitudes are a huge problem. Changes stemming from global warming are creeping up on us all so imperceptibly that the average person does not notice any difference in the day to day picture.

Swiss ferry near Interlaken

Consequently, when it may occasionally come to his or her notice, it is easier to push it to one side as being every one else's problem to solve and to act upon. In any case many people in the British Isles would say 'great' at the prospect of warmer weather, though even this prospect can receive a dent after a couple of colder-than-average winters, forming just a part of the cycle of the normal variations in our weather, only to be expected when arriving at an 'average' year. Such variations are all too easily latched onto by those sceptics who would deny scientific research about the upward trend of global warming. This must rank as a public relations ultimate worst nightmare.

Ready for take-off, Kombolcha, Ethiopia

An old Belfast tram set in a snowy garden

EXPENDING ENERGY

LEFT: Barry burning up energy in Singapore

BELOW: Lonely peacock seeks attractive peahen

Copenhagen fights for the planet

Oxen and farmer in Thailand

Manpower in a Venice backwater

Yet people can be jolted in their pockets by unexpected harsh realities, like a sudden steep rise in prices, especially oil and its derivatives, or the unavailability of some hitherto 'essential' item for the shopping trolley. I am not in any way qualified to offer solutions but my layman's words, backed by my photographs on some of the ecological aspects, may make at the very least an infinitesimal contribution to the picture we are all being forced to confront.

I must hold up my hand at this point and admit to being just as guilty as the next person over the carbon footprint I will have left behind me. Yet to those who would challenge me about this in the taking of the photographs in this book from so many countries, I reiterate that I was living, working and travelling on business in most of the countries depicted. Indeed many of the wonderful scenes and the people I saw were virtually outside my door, just as is every photo in Chapter 8. Many of my other Irish photos depict scenes within less than an hour's drive, generally combining some routine errand. Remember too that for all of my youth and until relatively recently the very expressions now in common use had not even been coined – like greenhouse gases, carbon trading, biofuels, renewable energy and the rest. We were all living in blissful ignorance of what we were doing to the entire planet. Yet even then there were voices crying in the wilderness, like Rachel Carson in her 1962 book *The Silent Spring*. How much graver things are today than even she foresaw. Hard truths that cannot be bypassed include the balance between energy supplies and rising demand (taking account of limited natural resources) and the escalating stress being placed on the natural environment.

This Cambodian girl had been washing lorries in a river.

Now let us look back almost 300 years. In the West Midlands in England is Ironbridge, created a World Heritage Site in 1986 to mark the area as the cradle of the Industrial Revolution. In and around this now beautiful gorge of the River

Horsepower, Ballyhornan

Thatching near Killinchy, Co. Down – c. 1970

Aleppo, Syria, in 1948

It takes two to look after eleven cygnets.

A winter walk by the Giant's Ring, Belfast

Cartwheeler and apprentice in Chester

Severn, there used to be many primitive blast furnaces producing steel, coal mining and attendant industries. The resultant concentrated pollution of air and land rendered the gorge more like some vision of Hell. Then came the first steps taken that led towards man's ability to affect the environment on a world scale.

Those brilliant industrialists, entrepreneurs, scientists, and engineers of the day unwittingly helped to bring us all to the tipping point the planet is facing today. They could hardly have imagined such a situation. Industrial development exploded and in its wake came great wealth, more jobs, higher standards of living – for some. Later came cars, aeroplanes, world travel around the 'global village' with its attendant benefits and the rampant consumerism now expanding across much of the world. We have all become what we are today largely by virtue of the amazing happenings which radiated out from that English river valley and its immediate environs.

An important physical link in the process was The Iron Bridge built in 1777 by Abraham Darby, a Quaker, the first cast iron bridge ever constructed and an object of wonder and beauty both in its earliest days and even today. It was built to overcome problems caused both by the Severn's great winter floods and currents and by the summer low water, each of which impeded essential travel across the river.

It is pure coincidence that this book is appearing on the eve of the December 2009 UN World Climate Change Conference in Copenhagen. I harbour hopes that some of those involved, either directly or indirectly, will find that this book might in some small way be an inspiration as they deliberate and subsequently, I trust, move urgently and effectively

The Iron Bridge, Shropshire, spans the Severn, England's longest river. Haven't we all great gulfs to bridge in the days ahead?

These young swallows nesting in an old tram, have to build up their energy to fly thousands of miles south in autumn.

Strangford Lough Regatta

THE SUN'S ENERGY IS FOR ALL THIS TOO

Bananas and flower in the tropics

Vines in France

Co. Armagh's famous app

ABOVE: Good friends really

RIGHT: Even jellyfish use energy

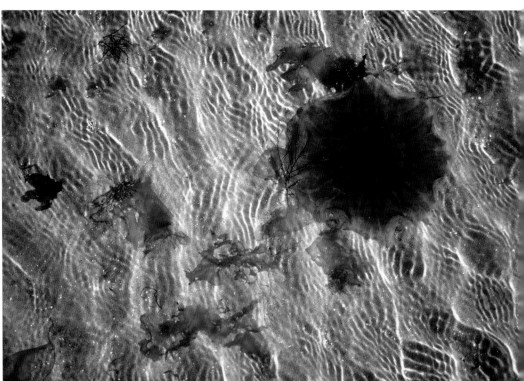

OPPO

Shafts of sunlight pierce the haze over John Lennon Airport, Liverpool,
local fuel source in the background – but modern travel is essen

POLLUTION

TOP LEFT: Pollution comes in many forms with an industrial haze creeping across Lake Como, Italy – but industry is essential.

MIDDLE LEFT: Smoke from home fires hangs over Dundrum (foreground) and Newcastle, Co. Down – but home heating is essential.

towards greater international cooperation and action in combating the survival problems the world faces. Indeed the whole book, with its fresh approach to weather and climate, could also provide some appropriate entertainment in moments of relaxation and travel. Certainly it is felicitous that several of my photographs depict wonderful Copenhagen in a favourable light.

Whatever you may think of my thoughts in this chapter especially, I do hope you will be able to delight with me in some of the wonders of God's creation and Man's handiwork across many lands, all of them brought to us, directly or indirectly, by the sun and the amazing weather it delivers to us – free. But there

is also a price to pay. The sun is not only a benefactor. It comes with a serious health warning attached – it burns the skin. Proof of this, if it were needed, is the large rise in skin-related problems confronted daily by the medical profession. My earlier photo of a prism therefore also carries with it another, more sinister, message. Yet sunshine in our north-western isles does noticeably cheer us up and in sensible small doses it gives us essential Vitamin D. Let's all enjoy it.

Last, but not least, rubbish and its proper disposal, from armchairs (photo page 10) to plastic and paper wrappers and to drinks cans, is my personal responsibility and everyone else's too – be it in city, town, village, sea, mountain top or countryside. Yes.

7

Enjoying the weather

I do, but certainly not always! My hope is that you too will derive more enjoyment from our daily dose of weather by the time you have read through this book, studied its photographs and thought about it beyond the usual 'Good morning, not a bad day'. Via keener observation you may even find the weather forecasts more interesting and relevant and be able to answer for yourself that burning question about whether or not to bring an umbrella. Or hang out the washing. Or go back to bed.

School break in Ballyconneelly, Co. Galway where I just love the feeling of the kids in the wide open spaces of the west.

In Hua Hin, Thailand, this Australian lady in a taxi was caught photographing Phyl and me in our taxi alongside, whilst I snapped them, to the typically Thai amusement of their taxi driver and his lady friend.

A laugh goes a long way, so amongst the photos in this chapter are a few to make you chuckle. Laughter and weather have this in common: they each come to us free of charge with no strings attached. And they know no international boundaries. Have a smile at some of the images that follow. Meanwhile look here at the faces of the four taxi occupants, taken from my taxi. Laughter is delightfully infectious.

I may be ridiculed for singing the praises of our Irish and British weather but just read again my reasons for extolling its virtues. But, you may ask, how can anyone, a farmer for example, possibly enjoy a really rotten day after days or weeks of the same? So take a look at some of the photos in this chapter and you should be encouraged by the good time apparently being enjoyed by all – or the stoicism being displayed in the weather of the occasion. Some days are best enjoyed in the recollection of them, like the relief of escaping with friends, frozen and soaked, into a good pub with a welcoming fire burning and a menu to match. Then while you are inside the sun breaks through and you can't wait to get out again – the air will be cool and fresh and every little stream will be gurgling.

Phyl and Kay on a wet walk by Wastwater, one of the most dramatic lakes in England's incomparable Lake District. Great Gable is the snow-capped peak in the centre, popular with climbers.

But what about those seemingly endless days of dull weather? Or the interminable cold, raw, penetrating, damp and the storms of mid-winter? They all do come to an end eventually and in the meanwhile there are endless enjoyable and useful ways of shutting out the gloom or the disappointment. Some handyman job around the house perhaps or sorting out a desk or drawer or garage that has been the subject of long procrastination. Very rewarding – I know the feeling! Then there is always your hobby or, dare I say it, the computer. Or there is always some housebound older person who would welcome a spot of company. Finally, a brisk walk in defiance of the elements after being cooped up indoors all day is wonderfully refreshing. Look too at the outdoor sports that continue despite the conditions, though usually more acceptable to the players than the spectators.

I rest my case. You cannot do anything to alter the day's weather, so make the most of it, good or bad. See what you think of this miscellaneous collection of 'Enjoying the Weather' photographs that follow.

It pays to advertise! Liverpool F. C. members will swell with pride to see this! Caught on camera in Portaferry, Co. Down, on a dull day with little else worth photographing on that annual outing of our camera club members.

On that same day in Portaferry Tom shares a laugh

Three lads at Al Ain camel market in the United Arab Republic wanted their picture taken and so did three Jewish lads on a day out in Prague in the Czech Republic

Liza is making the most of the sleepy afternoon heat in Chiang Mai, Thailand.

There have lately been some spells of truly atrocious weather when I have looked back over what I have written extolling the virtues of our weather – and I have begun to have misgivings … wondering: am I out of my mind? But I decided to stick to my guns. So let us all be unwavering, be it rain, snow, gale or shine and continue to make the best of what's on offer. And there is no use blaming the Met Office – or me.

A girl must at all times look her best! It was a truly dreadful day – cold, wet, windy – and now Marnie will be ready to face the world with confidence. Thanks Marnie.

LLANFAIRPWLLGWYNGYLLGOGERYCHWYRNDROBWLLLLANTYSILIO GOGOGOCH means The Church of Mary in the hollow of the white hazel near the fierce whirlpool and the Church of Tsolio by the red cave. I'm sure you knew this anyway, and how to pronounce it. Oh, that's my favourite model too. And, yes, it is Wales – Anglesey to be precise.

Probably most families have ageing photograph albums showing stiff groups of Victorian ancestors, but the coming of digital leads me to wonder whether copies of digitals will today find their way into family albums to entertain posterity with questions of incredulity like 'Did I really wear that?'

I wonder too whether some of the strangers from around the globe appearing in these pages will chance to spot themselves with some astonishment. My thanks go to them for their unwitting modelling and to friends and family who may or may not have been aware of my (sometimes covert, but harmless) camera activity.

Dog Simon with an appetite for knowledge and Michael, a judo casualty, make the most of a wet day in Singapore.

Now follows a random worldwide selection of people and animals enjoying the weather or indoors avoiding it. We all take shots like these for our own reasons and for sharing with friends and family. Indeed it is precisely photos such as these that have been the bread-and-butter of the photographic industry.

Summertime afloat – at the narrows between Strangford and Portaferry (background) enjoying the weather we all hope for.

A man in a Singapore lorry is highly amused at being photographed.

Bathers on a cold spring day enjoy a chat in a thermally heated pool in Reykjavik, Iceland.

The kiss, Funchal, Madeira

Boat manoeuvres in Strangford

Musicians in Prague, city of music

In Gracehill, a Moravian village near Ballymena, Co. Antrim

This girl was doing a photoshoot in Thailand – I joined in.

Count on a cat to find a sunny spot

LEFT
Linn Gardens, Argyllshire

Eleanor

CLOCKWISE FROM LEFT
Outdoor concert in the Tivoli Gardens, Copenhagen; Singapore Island Country Club offered swimming pool, golf, tennis – and curry puffs; on a windy hilltop are Alan, Jean and Phyl, with dog Emma, always the centre of attention; a warm summer's day at Portballintrae.

A glorious picnic spot above Zermatt

128   Relaxing in the grounds of Belfast's splendid City Hall

LEFT: Adrian and Amanda are appropriately launched.

BELOW LEFT: Liza, Lucy and Nuala are certainly not bored this wet day.

ABOVE: Corinne posing for yet another photograph – but seems to have mislaid the groom – already!

LEFT: Nine Thai girls, with lots of happy giggles and OKs grouped themselves like this for me.

Almost fifty years ago our kids used a derelict steamroller as a climbing frame in the jungle.

Enjoying Mount Stewart's magnificent gardens are John and Muriel.

RIGHT: Ryan, at Kilclief beach near our house – then and now with a mischievous thought lurking!

FAR RIGHT: Indian lads bake on the rocks at Batu Ferringhi, Penang. Most rocks in the tropics are curiously devoid of seaweed.

Teresa, a consistent winner at Strangford's annual Best Kept Garden Competition

Lorraine, always smiling in her Downpatrick shop.

Theo discovers poppies have no scent

RIGHT: 'I'll just let the blood drain back out of my tired, hot feet' thinks Anne Lise while Jørn just sits – Copenhagen.

LEFT
Alex

RIGHT
Theo, a few years later – spot the difference.

ABOVE: Phyl has The Pyramids almost to herself, Giza, near Cairo.

ABOVE LEFT: Haystacks, Co. Donegal, with Errigal in the background

Fun with shadows

ook at my nails', says Pamela.

RIGHT: Maurice, with camera, and Leslie share a joke at my expense.

MIDDLE RIGHT: Mia, in safe legs, with Mike and Marie, Ardgillan, Co. Dublin

FAR RIGHT: Liza and Jørn in Hua Hin, Thailand

Hauling in their nets, Mersing, West Malaysia

Our kids in a jungle riv

RIGHT: John and Hugh recapture their escaped sow – piglets imminent.

FAR RIGHT: Collecting rock oysters in the Singapore that was.

Sail training ship Lord
Nelson at anchor, Audley's
Roads, Strangford Lough

LEFT: coconuts, near Malacca, West Malaysia

BELOW: gambolling in a new white world

Trotting by

Thai hill tribe mother and child

Malaysian children

Thai woman
with a cheroot

Thai girl in a rice field

There's always something of interest for Michael, Joe and Isabel.

Margaret entertains Ricky and Caroline

ABOVE LEFT
Deirdre in red

CENTRE LEFT: Isabel and Dad doing gymnastics.

What a load of shopping and toddlers don't come cheap!

Fascination with machinery

Entertainment

More entertainment

8

Home skies, sea and more

Magnificent cumulus build-up looking east across Strangford Lough narrows.

Others might be living in their own paradise encompassing mountains, valleys, forests, great cityscapes, but here by the racing tides of Strangford Lough is my paradise, quite an intimate one, and I take pleasure in sharing it with you. Around 1,000 years ago I would have been sharing it with the many incursions of marauding Vikings – I wonder might I have some Viking blood in my veins?

This sea lough in County Down, with its 120 or so islands, sits at the most easterly edge of Ireland and is a clearly recognisable shape on TV weather maps. Because of its bottle-shape the currents at its narrow entrance stretching almost five miles are strong and eddying. Almost every week in the summer season we can see yachts not familiar with these waters sailing in against the tide, apparently at full speed if one is aboard, but actually losing momentum and sailing backwards; they often have to give up and await the turn of the tide. Because of its topography and its depths down to almost 200 feet it has a large range of habitats. Hence Strangford Lough is a haven for many kinds of wildlife, both resident and migratory, feeding on the riches found in the sea and along the varying shorelines at all seasons. The resident grey and common seals can be easily spotted, also occasionally otters, and these are joined in summer by more exotic visitors – porpoises, dolphins, and the odd basking shark or killer whale. Birdlife is a constant joy at all times, one of the most notable winter visitors being the world's largest gathering of white-bellied Brent geese. Hardly surprisingly the lough is a nature reserve of international significance.

Besides the scenery and the attractions of nature, Strangford Lough is also a haven for sailors of many kinds, canoeists, artists and not least those who simply want to sit and absorb the constantly changing scene through the seasons. Including me – indeed the view can be a terrible distraction from some job awaiting attention!

Vast and always on the move is how I can best describe 'my'

skies, extending as they do through 360 degrees, including a 15 degrees window to the open Irish Sea beyond Rock Angus, with its conspicuous tower. In that direction across the level horizon lie the mountains of Snowdonia in North Wales; whilst due to curvature of the Earth the land itself is below the horizon, I have on a few occasions of exceptional atmospheric conditions been able to discern the tops of cumulo-nimbus clouds over 100 miles away. Similarly, looking straight ahead eastwards across the Ards Peninsula I have seen the cloud tops over The Lake District; not half way there lies the Isle of Man, regularly to be seen from nearby and often with a line of cumulus clouds sitting over it.

The cloud shapes and the sky, the wind direction and strength, the time of day, and the state of the tide together combine to influence the fleeting colours of the sea, the rocky islands and the Ards Peninsula a mile or so away, while shades of colour and passing shadows bring life to the surrounding garden, fields, trees and banks of golden whins.

In this designated Area of Special Scientific Interest seals have their rights – and so do I!

My view provides an endless variety show of compelling interest throughout the seasons, in fair weather and in wild. But it is the indescribable beauty of it all that I find so utterly wonderful. I hope you will see what I mean in this small selection of the hundreds of photos I have taken here over more than 25 years, sensing something of the moment when my shutter went click.

One thing you will not see is a figure with camera occasionally prancing round the garden in pyjamas, even on a frosty morning, aiming to capture the right moment for a sunrise while the brief passing light effect still holds. Since no photographic record of this activity exists I will allow your imagination to toy with the spectacle. The only observers have been the wondrous ballet flights of winter birds, the busily feeding geese, a solitary heron, the garden birds hiding in the bushes, the occasional hare, seals on the rocks, the neighbouring cattle and sheep and perhaps the occupants of a distant passing boat. Only these last might have spotted with some bemusement, coupled with disbelief, this crazy nature-loving photographer-madman. I believe that there must be true dedication in the pursuit of a hobby. That is my excuse for such an unseemly display. So keep your eyes open!

St. Patrick's Country

It is along this narrow stretch of sea that Saint Patrick sailed in 432AD, making a chance landing just a few miles to the west by a stream near Saul. There he established Christianity in Ireland by converting a local chieftain. I try to conjure up the image of his craft passing by and wonder what the weather was like on that day, but one thing is certain; the tide was flooding, eddying amongst the treacherous rocks and islands. I know this because his crew could never have succeeded in sailing in against an ebb tide. It was the Vikings a few hundred years later who gave this stretch the name 'strong fiord', this in time becoming Strangford Lough. So it was that same tide I daily see, which swept in the man who was to become the patron saint of Ireland. Hence the whole Lecale area reaching 10 miles westwards to Downpatrick, the traditional grave of the saint alongside Down Cathedral, has become known as St. Patrick's Country. Lecale is filled with archaeological and other remains and is steeped in the history and legend of Patrick to be discovered among an exciting network of winding roads. This postcard of mine proves it!

CLOCKWISE FROM TOP LEFT

St. Patrick's Statue, near Raholp; Saul Church on a site of Christian worship going back to Patrick's time; Cloghy Rocks, past which the saint sailed into Strangford Lough; River Quoile, lying between Patrick's landing place in 432AD and his grave in Downpatrick. These last two are Nature Reserves of outstanding interest and beauty.

The best way to share with you my skies and what lies beneath them is to take you on a clockwise journey from my house. Most of the photographs speak for themselves. However here and there I add a few words for your better appreciation of the whole picture and all the elements that combine to form the moving kaleidoscope, comprising land, sea, sky, wildlife and passing craft.

Do, I suggest, bring your binoculars but you should not need an umbrella since this area is not only one of the sunniest, but also one of the lowest rainfall zones in all Ireland. Time and again I see great build-ups of clouds apparently heading our way but they either disperse or else they pass us by on either side, especially when I know my garden needs a good watering. And if by mischance it were to rain your umbrella would probably be blown inside out anyway! Take my word for it.

The photographs that follow were taken over many years through 360 degrees around the compass. You will first be looking North and North-east, then East and South-east, then South and South-west and finally West and North-west. Because of the telephoto effect in some of the photos you will have the impression that you are looking through binoculars – which is precisely what I do every day, perhaps to look at seals or birds or at the waves at the bar mouth where the waters of Strangford Lough join the open Irish Sea. All these photos were shot from my house and garden or from a few yards away.

I hope you will enjoy this small patch of paradise with me, not least the skies and the fickle, maddening, uplifting and ever-changing weather, reflected in the colours and textures of the sea below, never dull for long but just working up to the next surprise treat for us. 'My' sea at the bottom of the garden is a highway to every other coastline on the planet. A pretty astounding thought on which end this chapter.

LOOKING NORTH TOWARDS PORTAFERRY

When you look at my pictures to the north you will notice a prominent tower on a hilltop – it is the stump of an old windmill dominating Portaferry across the narrows of Strangford Lough, familiar to me since earliest childhood when I regularly visited relations there. I still do. On Christmas Day 1878 disaster struck when the windmill was totally destroyed in a fire, begun in a way that was not uncommon among the

numerous old windmills round the area. The miller had apparently failed to tether the sails properly when he went down to the town for a Christmas drink, so when a great wind blew up the sails churned wildly around so the wooden bearings overheated with the friction and soon caught alight. It must have been an appalling shock, not just to the unfortunate miller but to all the local people who will have seen the towering inferno on the hilltop, where there would have been no easy access to water to fight the blaze. In recent years some restoration was undertaken to save the building from collapsing, so we on the Strangford side of the water enjoy this conspicuous landmark as well as the Portaferry folk. The windmill is the most significant of a number of interesting old buildings I can see in every direction, including two castles, four churches and ever so many footprints of ancient history and of the Anglo-Normans.

LOOKING EAST TOWARDS THE ARDS

TOP RIGHT

The first sight of the sun ushering in
the new millenium in Ireland

Our nearest neighbours

143

A parade of vessels involved in installation
of SeaGen (p.108)

ABOVE

The 'Hebridean Princess', a former Scottish inter-island ferry, now a luxury cruise vessel

ABOVE RIGHT

Beyond the yachts is a significant whirlpool, the Routen Wheels.

RIGHT

Herons are always around, while cormorants crown Cloghy Rocks beacon.

Towards the Bar Mouth – a violent storm raises spindrift.

CONTINUING TO LOOK SOUTH

RIGHT

A rare sight of cumulus mammatus below a thunderstorm – highly dangerous to aircraft.

BELOW

'Rambiz' crane barge enters the lough bringing SeaGen (the black column).

BOTTOM LEFT

An evening hail shower

We call this Willow Pond;
it has quite a range of
freshwater birds.

LOOKING WEST – INLAND

9

A journey from Box Brownie to digital

Like countless others of my vintage my photography began with a Christmas present of a Kodak Box Brownie when I was about eleven. Here are some of my earliest photos (1938–41), each with a pretty tenuous weather connection, though that did not enter my young head at the time.

Drumbeg Lock on the Lagan Canal some five miles south of Belfast. Horse-drawn barges were then a slow but reliable and economical (and environmentally friendly) mode of freight transport – coal, timber and other building materials to Lough Neagh, with sand and gravel on the return trip. One very happy boyhood recollection is of being allowed to put my bicycle on a barge as it crunched its way through the overnight ice that had formed on the canal, with the horse's breath rising in the crisp morning air over the towpath. I wish I had a photo of that, but in those days a camera was not carried around everywhere in the way it is today; anyway film was expensive and my weekly 6d (i.e. 2.5p) pocket money would not have stretched that far. Life seemed much less frenetic then, and certainly for kids, much freer than it is today.

This line-up of steamers viewed from Belfast's Queen's Bridge always filled me with excitement as they lay ready for their overnight crossing to England and Scotland, which seemed another world away. They were not of course car ferries and the walk up the steep gangway was the ultimate thrill. It was quite often the case that one would first notice the heaving of the vessel as it emerged from the shelter of Belfast Lough, then the swish and thump of the waves against the hull as one snatched some sleep. Half way, as the ship rounded the Isle of Man it would alter course and the motion would be noticeably different. Arrival in Britain could often be an anti-climax as the docks seemed cold and dreary in the early morning light and suitcases heavy as one lugged them to the train.

Wartime meant strict rationing of most food and 'Dig for Victory' became the catchphrase, so parts of gardens everywhere were dug up for vegetables, while in the suburbs people also kept hens to provide a great supply of eggs – like my mother here and Phyl's mother across the road.

As a mad keen amateur my aspiration has always been the achieving of at least a good photographic recording of what appeals to me, much of it in the natural world around us. I therefore aim at a reasonable, and if possible unusual, photograph that any person with an eye to see it is perfectly capable of taking. Indeed I would like your reaction to many of my photos to be: 'I could take just as good a one as that! Or better!' However I must confess here to having done little of my own processing. In 1952 I struggled with black & white developing and printing while I was living in Nigeria, but critical temperature control in that steamy climate without air-conditioning was a sweaty nightmare.

So I decided there and then to leave the messy technical work to the professionals. I am sure that in any case I did not have the patience for that essential aspect of photography, hence I suppose some would label me a pseudo-photographer. So be it. But I am in good company. The late Wilfred Thesiger, explorer and photographer extraordinaire admitted to the same approach as mine. Also, I feel an unusual bond with him for he was born in Ethiopia as was Deirdre our first child, British birth No. 99 there.

As I relied on professionals I would like to pay special tribute to three of them who were particularly helpful to me along life's photographic way. There was Mr Der Simonian in Beirut, from 1948 to 1952 in my earliest days abroad.

Here he is with a clerical friend, a fellow Armenian, in a monastery in the Lebanon.

Then there was Hock Cheong in Singapore in the 1960s; and finally Esler Crawford and his team in Belfast from the 1980s. There were lean years in the 1950s in Ethiopia and Nigeria when I had no such personalised professional help. Esler once gave me a great piece of advice: if you find yourself faced with some unique and fantastic photo opportunity that may never present itself again, don't stint yourself on film. The discipline that has to accompany this is being ruthless in throwing out the less than perfect shots. With the coming of digital photography and memory cards the advice to shoot away does not have the same meaning. But the need to be ruthless in eliminating junk is even more essential. As for photographic equipment my requirements have been simple and I changed cameras but rarely. It was not until 1946 that I went upmarket and bought a second-hand Kodak bellows-type for £4, a sum I found it hard to spare; in 1950, when I was working in the Middle East and could afford the luxury, came a brand new gleaming Zeiss Ikon Super Ikonta, referred to simply as Z in letters home to my family. Z accompanied me everywhere.

This was taken in Petra, Jordan, on Z's first outing. It was also my first and only photo taken while on horseback, the best way by far of approaching this wondrous and remote place lost amongst dramatic sandstone mountains, and only revealed to the Western world when it was discovered in 1812 by Swiss Johann Burckhardt. I was there in 1950 with two Palestinian colleagues, long before Petra became familiar on the tourist trail. Yet this angle on the Pharaoh's Treasury will never change as it comes dramatically into view after winding through a long narrow gorge, the Sik. That famous phrase of Petra being 'a rose-red city half as old as time' is surely one of the most apt that has ever been used. The excitement of our short visit – we were actually en route to Aqaba on business (how I suffered!) – was heightened when a monumental thunderstorm broke beyond the encircling mountains but without a single drop of rain falling on us. When we emerged we discovered that the nearby desert was white with hail. It was a far cry from the searing heat of summer on another occasion en route to Aqaba when we encountered a man begging for water by the side of the track. Yes, water. The village where we hired our steeds for the mile-long ride is the reputed place where Moses struck the rock on the command of God and water flowed to quench the thirst of the Israelites on their long journey out of Egypt in this seemingly harsh and lifeless place. Biblical history is everywhere here.

SC3948 appeared in a calendar of old Singapore cars after we left – with a Singaporean Chinese beauty draped delectably over the bonnet! The open top has weather tales to tell – either struggling to erect the hood against a sudden monsoon deluge, or the day I was driving along happily with hood in position in the torrents and it flew back and left me drenched in seconds, to the hilarity of other motorists. I had omitted to tighten the two butterfly nuts securing it. A much loved car.

In 1956 in Addis Ababa I changed to a Kodak Retina IIIc, a handy size of camera and a classic still in working order with no fancy electronics to go wrong and no batteries to run out at some critical moment. Then in the mid-1960s I bought a Canon SLR with a fixed 50mm lens which did me fine for many years, until its demise when I fell headlong into a jungle river and had to replace it with the same again. But in the 1990s I yielded to the taunts of my camera club friends and bought a similar Canon with a built-in 28–90mm lens. This is what I have today, an EOS300 for slide work, though even this has virtually petered out with the advent of my digital camera.

Yes, digital! It was in late 2004 that I succumbed to pressure from my younger son Michael and bought a Sony digital compact box of tricks which, I have to admit, is quite incredible. But I do not like over-use of its amazing facilities for enhancement, though the correcting of crooked horizons and judicial use of cropping are most useful tools. Indeed I have always been what I would term a purist i.e. I maintain that a photograph should, where possible, be correctly composed and exposed at the moment of taking without having to resort to manipulation to achieve the desired result. After all, how can we, how dare we, try and improve on nature's colours, for instance? I know that many will not go along with my purist approach, and that is their privilege. But now for a complete diversion with positively no tampering, our wonderful 1950s Morris Minor tourer loaded with the kids ready for school in Singapore.

On all my travels I have never carried accoutrements like additional lenses, tripod etc. though as a one-time Boy Scout I learned to 'Be Prepared', so I always had spare films with me. However with my self-imposed restriction in paraphernalia I have had to accept that my range of photographic possibilities has been significantly narrowed, but the huge advantage of simplicity has, for me, far outweighed this. Indeed this is probably a very good thing otherwise my cupboards would have been even more cluttered with negatives, slides, prints of all sizes etc. than they already are. The reader can judge whether my images justify my policy of always travelling light. Digitals though are the ultimate in convenience.

As to type of film, in my early days I used only Kodak Verichrome black & white and indeed until I took to digital I always stuck faithfully to Kodak. I progressed from B&W to Kodachrome colour slide film in 1962 when the only available speed was the rather slow ASA25. This could pose problems with camera shake when hand-held in conditions of poor light such as deep forest, overcome at times by using my walking stick as a camera prop in lieu of tripod. Eventually ASA200 became a vast improvement for the keen amateur, though this has now fallen victim to digital. The quality of my slides taken on Kodachrome film almost fifty years ago is still as good as the day they were taken. Look for example at this shot taken in Singapore in the mid-1960s showing men at work on sailing ships from the Celebes (now Sulawesi) in Indonesia.

There was a period for perhaps 15 years until the advent of my digital that I also used a certain amount of colour print film, largely family shots, on a miniature camera, the main one being an Olympus mju, for convenience of sharing copies with the family.

The none too subtle filial pressure that I should move into the 21st Century means that I now use almost exclusively an extremely convenient pocket-sized Sony digital camera. I do not ever see myself progressing (?) to photography by mobile phone even though I see my youngest grandchildren, barely able to point a camera, taking at least passable photos with one. I even wonder whether photography has not now evolved into something almost too casual, too easy, rather than the art form that it should be, though this aspect will always remain. What next? Harnessing the blink of an eye? What a phenomenal revolution in photography since 1835 when Henry Fox Talbot took the earliest surviving paper negative photograph depicting an oriel window in Lacock Abbey, Wiltshire. I show here my digital photo of that window.

Over the past thirty years I have from time to time put my photographs to use in various ways, such as by raising money for charities through talks with slide shows and by photo exhibitions. Also, after some prodding by a cousin, I have produced a series of high quality landscape postcards of Northern Ireland, a not too serious and certainly not very lucrative semi-retirement occupation. I concentrated on what might be termed the tourist honey spots, though not exclusively. Over the years I have produced around 200 different cards and sold almost two million that have winged their way across the world, helping in a small way to promote a more positive image of Northern Ireland during a black period in history when it seemed that only bad news was coming from here. A rather satisfying thought.

Lacock Abbey window from the outside – Fox Talbot's photo was taken from inside.

One of two special postcards, each varying the theme 'This is the **real** Northern Ireland'. The caption on reverse reads, clockwise from top left: A road in the Mournes; ancient carved figures on White Island, Lower Lough Erne, Co. Fermanagh; Belfast's Cavehill Road; Atlantic breakers near Portballintrae, Co. Antrim.

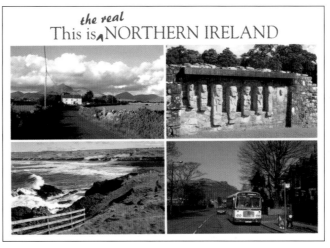

Irish Hen Party – taken near Malin Head, Co. Donegal

I have regarded each of my postcards as a kind on mini art piece just as every photograph should aim to be – not that that ever occurred to me in my early days with a camera. Here is my most successful postcard and positively not a posed shot – I defy anyone to get a hen to perch on a chair like that!

Bird's eye view of Strangford.

As you may have noticed, I often have my camera handy while flying as I enjoy gazing down and trying to understand from a different perspective the land forms and all the activity going on down there. Here is an aerial view looking northwards to Strangford Village on its peninsula, with the ferry approaching harbour from Portaferry. At high tide I can row around the islands in the lower left. This fondness for looking down at what lies below is undoubtedly related to my love of maps and atlases; some people have a phobia about these and rejoice in today's GPS as being completely dependable when driving — mostly, but not always!

So that, then, is my very unsophisticated 'technical' and 'commercial' photographic story. I have had and still derive endless satisfaction and enjoyment from this unique and wonderful hobby of photography which I still pursue energetically alongside watercolour painting, which I took up almost by accident — but that is another story involving my lucky escape from a major air disaster.

In the Introduction I said that in the quest for a photograph I had even suffered indignities. I must therefore confess the following in case any reader might have been an eye-witness: One fine morning after a good breakfast at a B&B in Ballycastle, Co. Antrim, I turned into a scenic cliff-edge car park to get a different photo angle on Sheep Island, but in order to see it properly I had to squeeze through a barbed wire fence onto a perfectly safe wide ledge on the other side. In order not to entangle my camera strap in the barbed wire I threw it across onto the soft grass and proceeded to follow it beyond the fence. At least I tried to. Whatever ham-fisted way I tackled the fence I somehow managed to get my trousers fiercely entangled in the barbed wire, and the more I struggled the worse things became. I might have succeeded in extricating myself but at the cost of shredding a perfectly good pair of trousers. Anyway I had no spare trousers. What's more my camera had landed just out of reach. So there was only one solution – to wriggle somehow out of my trousers. I was at the far side of a deserted scenic car park at a time when no one in their right senses would have wanted to park there. So I squirmed and twisted, nearly dislocating my back, eventually parting from my trousers, leaving them impaled on the barbed wire, without losing too much blood in the process. Having quickly retrieved my camera I saw with disgust that the photo of the island was not worth taking! So I crawled over to the offending fence, carefully disentangled my precious trousers, threw them back to the car park side, clambered very cautiously back – and rapidly made myself respectable again. The moral of the story is: Treat barbed wire fences with respect even if they do not actually say 'Cliff Edge' or 'Keep Out' or even 'Beware of the Bull'. Another moral perhaps – no photographer, however zealous, should go forth without spare trousers. Here is the non-photo that could have cost me my reputation.

???

One concluding thought to leave with you – it is that word *unique.* Have you ever paused to consider that virtually every one of the trillions of photographs that have ever been taken is, even in just some infinitesimal way, totally unique? So too every snowflake. Every cloud. Every tidal pond. Every creature. And so much more. Us. As that old French actor, singer and entertainer Maurice Chevalier once said, referring to the difference between the sexes: 'Vive la différence!' (Long live the difference!) Think about uniqueness. The God-given world is unimaginably full of uniqueness to be enjoyed by all those who can see and appreciate it. And it is there to be seen through the lens and to be recorded for posterity – like these parting shots of mine.

What could be more transient or unique than bubbles and the simple delight they bring?

Or any flower or tree or this carpet of maple leaves in Canada?

155

And only I saw this beach array of stones, shells and sand, soon to be rearranged with the next tide.

Skirting an evening thunderstorm before touching down in Singapore – never another quite the same

And how could this pattern of clouds and treetops ever be replicated?

Taking a break lying on my back gazing at little puffs of summer clouds gradually dissolving.

And what about this cobweb drooping with overnight dew and useless as a flytrap – I wonder if spiders have the mental capacity to find this frustrating?

Twins and their doubles, Ardglass

What a range of emotions can flit momentarily across the face and interact so tellingly with another person of any age – or animal.

Now, finally, to bid you farewell I share this corona round the moon, taken from my window.

As the sun dips behind the Mournes on 1 February 2008 at 4.43pm (so my laptop tells me and it couldn't possibly be wrong!) there is a noticeable lengthening of the days, and while winter is by no means over, spring is just around the corner – and I have never heard anyone object to that.

HAPPY PHOTOGRAPHY TO ALL, YOUNG AND NOT SO YOUNG – WITH OR WITHOUT UMBRELLA!

A lifeboat story with a difference

Lifeboats and weather go together, so one's mind has an image of a craft in distress in a raging storm at sea, with the nearest RNLI lifeboat dashing to the rescue. But there are countless other emergencies to which RNLI (Royal National Lifeboat Institution) crews respond – without regard to their own personal safety. They cover the long indented coastline right round Britain and Ireland plus the offshore islands and many inland waterways 24 hours per day – 365 days a year in all weathers.

I have a most unusual reason for this addendum to my book just before it goes to print. First, though, let me tell you of our local RNLI lifeboat, always ready to come to my aid when I am out in my 9-foot dinghy, perhaps with my grandchildren, or maybe cut off by in incoming tide, or even in an emergency involving our local car-ferry. Perish the thought. Here are some photographs of the Portaferry lifeboat, stationed across the narrows about a mile from my home.

The new state-of-the-art Atlantic 85 inshore lifeboat 'Blue Peter V' shows off its paces between Portaferry and Strangford after launching by tractor at the slip across the road opposite the exciting new Lifeboat Station. In its first week it was called out 3 times to answer distress calls. Its predecessor in Portaferry, one of the busiest stations in Ireland, chalked up 325 emergency calls over 16 years, rescuing a total of 353 people, not just within Strangford Lough but in the nearby open Irish Sea. The treacherous currents, many islands, hidden rocks, fogs and wild gales make the whole area particularly hazardous for the thousands of people who enjoy all the delights the lough has to offer, especially from Easter to October.

But what has this got to do with this addendum you may be asking? I now explain. I have only just learned, incredibly, of the probable involvement of a lifeboat crew in helping to save my life in January 1989. I had been flying from London to Belfast when, at cruising altitude, the aircraft developed serious engine trouble. It was diverted to East Midlands Airport but it crashed just short of the runway onto the M1 Motorway near Kegworth. An RNLI crew from Withernsea, Yorkshire, happened to be passing along the M1 and promptly joined in the rescue along with an army of firemen, medics and other rescuers. .

The crew's particular involvement, apparently, was in helping to remove casualties through the broken fuselage and across the aircraft's wing – and that is how I was extracted after being trapped for a couple of hours. I was in a sorry state and barely conscious, but I was lucky – I survived where 47 didn't. Amidst all the chaos at the scene, involving so many branches of the emergency services, there is no way of knowing for sure that it was the RNLI that stretchered me to a waiting ambulance. At any rate, there they were in action when they were needed, right in the middle of England and far from the sea. That says it all about the RNLI.

I have already met and thanked the airport firemen and others involved in the rescue and its aftermath – hospital staff, padre and others. But this story is my way, however unorthodox, of saying a belated thank you (but better late than never) to the crew of the Withernsea lifeboat whose involvement I have just heard of by chance.

RNLI crews, all volunteers and backed by public support, undergo rigorous training on a regular basis to enable them to handle a wide range of emergencies, sometimes working with other branches of the emergency services – but they can scarcely have been prepared for the scenes that confronted them that grim winter evening on England's M1. At least the weather was good that night – it was dry and cool.

Published by Booklink
Publisher: Dr Claude Costecalde, Booklink,
120 High Street, Holywood, Co Down, BT18 9HW

© Photographs Alan Johnston
© Text, Alan Johnston, 2009

Design by Wendy Dunbar, Ireland
Printed in Slovenia

ISBN 978-1-906886-21-9